Wealth Building NO

10 Principles for Wealth Building Success in a Post-COVID-19 Environment

Wealth Building NOW

Library of Congress Cataloging-in-Publication Data

ISBN: 978-1-953994-22-6

Publisher: TFA Financial Planning

Wealth Building NOW provides you a concise and to the point guide on how you and others can use **10 success principles** to build wealth and have comprehensive effectiveness as you manage your finances—an opportunity to do just that more precisely at this time.

Printed in the United States of America

Self-Published

Text design by Thomas (TJ) Underwood

ISBN: 978-1-953994-22-6

Wealth Building NOW

10 Guiding Principles for Wealth Building Success in Any Economic Environment

Success formulas for those who are NOW willing to give it their best:

1) **Adversity**—*You must always respond positively to adversity*

2) **Character**—*You must operate with character at all times*

3) **Excellence**—*You must have a track record of doing what you need to do, and you want to excel and work toward making your dreams come true*

4) **Imagination**—*You must have the ability to dream big and take action*

5) **Focus**—*You must zoom in on and pursue what you desire most with laser like focus*

6) **Confidence**—*You must know within your mind and heart that you desire to set yourself apart*

7) **Control**—*You must know at all times that if you do what you need to do, you can control your outcomes and make your dreams come true*

8) **Creativity**—*You must know how to use your creativity to achieve even more*

9) **Determination**—*Your determination level will determine if you really want the wealth building success that you are pursuing*

10) **Destiny**—*Your destiny will be determined by the actions that you take on a consistent basis*

Appendix A

Appendix B

Appendix C

You can "ace" your understanding of wealth building "if" you have the confidence, control, creativity, and determination to reach your destiny!

Once you combine the success formula or 10 principles (inside your mind and heart) and you decide to give it your absolute best consistently, you will begin to synergistically achieve major success and build wealth at a level that is your absolute best!

Introduction

Over the years I have written about many topics as it relates to personal finance and wealth building. In this timely book, **10 of the most important principles** that can guide you toward wealth building success will be presented to help you and others who desire to build wealth more effectively and efficiently an opportunity to do just that.

And with the planned release of this book occurring roughly 10 years from the date of formulation and creation of **TheWealthIncreaser.com** website, this book has special meaning in more ways than one.

Wealth Building NOW!!! *10 Guiding Principles for Wealth Building Success in Any Economic Environment* is designed to inspire and uplift those who desire to achieve wealth building success in a more effective manner so that the goals that they desire most can come into fruition in a timelier manner.

It is important that you utilize your mind in a manner that is of high intensity and is focused on the success that you desire. Your daily focus must be so strong that the success that you desire is the "only" possible outcome!

You must ask yourself "what can I use" to help reach my goals more efficiently and effectively and how can I achieve <u>winning success</u> in all areas of my finances?

You must imagine yourself being unstoppable in your pursuit toward the wealth building success that you desire—and using your mind diligently to look at your finances from a fresh new perspective that is not the norm could be what is needed in your life that can turn your current situation into that of greater success.

By asking and answering the **"right questions"** you can help bring what you visualize and sincerely want in your and your family's future—into reality!

In Wealth Building NOW you will be able to analyze what you can do to work toward building wealth in a more responsible and rewarding manner where your and your family's success is at the forefront!

It is important that you draw up in your mind a **realistic outlook** of how you will get to where you want to go as you journey toward **building your wealth** more intelligently.

You no longer must ask— "Can I" manage my finances and achieve the wealth building success that I need and/or desire. The question soon will be, will I manage my finances more effectively now that I possess the knowledge that is needed to do just that?

Asking and answering the right questions stimulates your thought process and provides your mind with new insight on accomplishing your future goals.

Below you will learn what you can do **right now** to work toward achieving your future goals and **building wealth** in a more efficient manner.

- **Focus On Success by Having a Realistic Plan for Achieving Success**

Do you know what your monthly income and expenses are, and do you know what you spend monthly?

Your monthly discretionary income is the starting point to getting you in position to achieve lasting success in your **building of wealth.**

You cannot have a **half-hearted** approach or just go through the motions. You must put a **solid written plan** in place and do your absolute best to follow through with that solid plan by doing what is necessary on a consistent basis!

Even those who currently have a **high net worth** could achieve far more if only they had an effective system in place that allowed them to manage their monthly income and expenses in a more intelligent, consistent, smarter and more beneficial manner.

By creating a **realistic plan for success,** you will know your monthly income and your monthly expenses and you will have an understanding **within your mind** of how to manage your income and expenses effectively so that you can reach your desired goals.

By knowing your income and expenses monthly, you can put a plan in place that will allow you to reach your future goals in a realistic way and not just base your future goals on wishful thinking or improper planning.

You want to **build wealth** in a manner where you have a properly funded emergency fund and little or no credit card debt and a comprehensive understanding of your finances. In **Appendix B** you will be presented with a wealth building approach that provides all that so that you can position yourself for success throughout your lifetime!

- **Use Proper Wealth Building Strategies to Reach Your Desired Goals**

By utilizing a <u>monthly cash flow statement (budget)</u> you can pursue your future goals with more focus and commitment and **build wealth** in a more effective manner because you will know your "financial numbers" and you will be in a better position to see your future more clearly and reach your desired goals.

Setting <u>meaningful and significant goals</u> and creating a pathway to reaching those goals that are realistic and based on your own unique monthly income and expenses are critical for you and your family **<u>if you are sincere</u>** in really reaching your goals.

Keep in mind that due to life events or other factors that you may not have control over, you may have to modify your goals and/or the timetable for reaching them. However, you must not be discouraged, and you must continue to move toward the goals that you desire to attain.

You must balance your goals and at the same time use wisdom in your approach.   It is important that you look at your finances in a comprehensive manner—even while creating your budget and establishing your emergency fund, as it will help immensely in your goal setting efforts.

Insurance Planning, Investment Planning, Tax Planning, Education Planning, Estate Planning/Wills and Retirement Planning will all come into clearer focus once you create a monthly budget and you know the amount of your <u>discretionary income</u> that you have left over so that you can achieve your other goals

In addition to learning the **10 principles** in the body of this book, in the bonus section you will learn an **"Investment Simplification Approach"** that will provide you the opportunity to reach targeted amounts that you plan for so that you can enjoy life more abundantly.

Therefore, you at this time want to approach your **wealth building efforts** with a "mindset of comfort" as you will have a highly effective system that allows you to build wealth effectively once you complete the reading of this book.

- **Build Your Wealth Intelligently**

You must realize that the more diverse your investment mix—the more the odds are that your plan will stand the test of time. Consider index funds as well as actively managed funds, CD's, <u>I-bonds and other bonds</u> and money market accounts, and be sure that you are comfortable and have a real understanding of how what you are investing in works.

Be sure to use tax-advantaged accounts and tax advantaged contributions to your maximum benefit!

And above all decide right now—and know within your mind and heart that **<u>the time to seriously approach your finances and achieve your dreams</u>**—will NEVER be just right!

By deciding to take control of your **Wealth Building** future **<u>right NOW</u>**—you can put yourself in position to control your future and **<u>increase your returns</u>** and do what you really want to do during your lifetime—and at the same time you minimize letting others control your future and enhancing their bottom line at your expense.

Now is the time that you use your creativity and insight (ideas, theories, models, <u>inspiration,</u> concepts, goals, <u>dreams,</u> etcetera) and this book—to move forward and get your future right.

*By **building your wealth** in a more thoughtful and intelligent manner you can achieve much more in your future!*

You will soon possess ideas and insight within your mind and heart that will put you within reach of making your and your family's future a much more prosperous one.

*You will soon be able to do far more to work toward **building your and your family's wealth** and achieve much more during your lifetime.*

Always remember that if you desire to **build your wealth** more effectively, you must have a system (within your mind) that allows you to <u>create a personal budget, create a personal income statement and create a personal balance sheet and you must know your personal net worth at this time</u>—so that you can get <u>MOMENTUM</u> rolling—if you are to achieve at your highest levels.

You must then use the information that is derived from those statements as a major tool to help you formulate **<u>written goals</u>** that can make a real and lasting difference in your life and lead you and your family forward in **building wealth** in a more efficient manner than if you had not done so.

You must make up your mind at this time to really pursue (take the right action on a daily basis) what you desire in your future with all of your might and every fiber in your body!

Now is the time that you dig deep and stretch your mind and heart further than you've ever stretched before—**by doing so the success that you always dreamed of will be just behind the door!**

That success will be due in large part to the **decision that you made** to open your mind up to what was possible and looking at your future in a more engaging and prosperous manner so that you could **build your wealth** in a more intelligent, consistent and proactive manner.

Wealth Building NOW wishes to introduce you and your family to a more successful path to future success where roadblocks are minimized or non-existent.

It is particularly important in the times that we now live in that you live your life with "high standards" as a major benchmark in your life.

Even if you are currently very successful in your credit and financial life you need to operate from the perspective that the success that you now enjoy can be improved upon. You should want to take your success to a higher state, whether it be financial or otherwise!

Even though you may appear successful in your own eyes and in the eyes of others, there is always room for improvement.

However, you and your family should be commended for reaching your current level of success. By having a real determination to further pursue success at a level that is your absolute best, you have made a "major decision" to put procrastination to rest.

Your goal should always be to operate with high standards and pursue excellence by doing your "absolute best" at what you do—or plan to do!

By doing so you take your mental state to a higher level!

If you try to excel in all areas of your credit, financial and everyday life you bring the possibility for increased success in your and your family's life.

In **Wealth Building NOW**, I have **tried to excel** at providing you **10 principles of wealth building** to help you improve your credit, finance, and real estate pursuits in the most efficient and effective manner possible.

By reading and applying what you will soon learn you can use the advice and information to change your future in a major way and achieve lasting goals.

The information and advice in this book are for those who "sincerely" want to change their wealth building future in a major way—in a comprehensive, highly effective and highly efficient manner!

You must make it a point to **operate at a high level of excellence** in all that you do if your goal is to be successful at a very high level.

You must set the bar high and reach higher in your life!

Make it a point at this time to do your absolute best at what you are doing or plan to do!

You can't depend on others to take you to where you need or want to be, because the destiny that you see or will soon see is only meant for you—and who you were truly meant to be.

Excelling at a high level requires that you actually want to be among the best at what you do!

If you are in the process of improving your credit and finances, you want to do your absolute best at attaining those goals!

You must have the attitude that you will **excel at your highest level** while you are on <u>your journey to reaching your goals</u> for yourself and your family.

It is important that you are <u>"properly prepared"</u> and you have the <u>"proper focus"</u> if you want to **excel at a high level.**

Excellence and high standards are required if you want to reach your credit, financial and life goals!

Don't live your life in a manner where you accept mediocrity and less than your best in all that you do!

Excellence is a quality that you must always aspire to attain!

You can have a successful, prosperous future if you **set your standards high** and you **operate at a high level of excellence** daily!

Be sure to <u>aim high</u>, <u>have meaningful and beneficial goals for yourself and your family</u> and **do your best to excel** in all that you engage in.

Your **personal standards** should be at such a high level that nothing that the outside world will say or do—will affect you in a negative way!

Quite the contrary, negative comments by others will provide a high level of <u>inspiration</u> and <u>motivation</u> for you if you have the right approach for success!

Now <u>is the time</u> to ask **Why!** Now is the Time to set the bar **High!** By doing so <u>You can exceed the **Sky!**</u>

Be sure to set meaningful and inspiring goals and do your absolute best to reach those goals.

You must set the bar high if you are to exceed the sky!

You must reach down in your soul, muster up the strength to reach your goal—and know that success in all that you do will be a lifetime role!

Go out and make your dreams come true—**Wealth Building NOW** provides you a road map of what you can <u>NOW</u> do—to see your way through!

Acknowledgements

This book is the result of all the people that have been a part of my life since birth and have had a major influence on my life whether personal, business, social or any other area—as they have all played a role and helped in the creation of much of this timely book.

Chapter 1

Adversity—*You must always respond positively to adversity*

Adversity or unwanted happenings during your lifetime will occur, regardless of who you are or how effectively you plan for your future.

And because of the importance of always responding positively to adversity, it is not only included in this book, but is also the first principle introduced as it is key to your long-term success, whether for the building of wealth or attaining success in other areas of your life.

Even though the best of planning can't prevent adversity and unwanted happenings from occurring in your life, you still want to do all that you can to manage and respond appropriately to adversity and other unwanted occurrences that occur throughout your life, in the best manner possible.

As the news on a daily basis can be depressing to many and lead them to have a more pessimistic view of their future, it is important that you do all that you can to stay positive and know that your wealth building dreams will come true.

In this chapter you will be presented with steps that you can take to "respond positively to adversity" so that you can achieve more throughout your lifetime.

And just as I've had to dig in, and discover new ways to move forward <u>when adversity of a high magnitude occurred</u>—so too must you do the same.

In the following paragraphs you will learn ways that you can face adversity in a manner where you can move forward as opposed to going backward, remaining where you are at—or possibly remaining in a depressed state for a prolonged period.

Respond to Adversity in a Winning Style

Despite the pain that you will often face because of major life events, it is not the end of the world, and you can take actions that can move you forward.

When you face adversity, remember that generally no one else cares.

Always remember that with adversity—how you got to where you are is not as important as where you can and need to go, even when it is not your fault, however the solution to move forward and overcome any adversity that you face is up to you!

At a time of grief, it can often be very difficult to move forward effectively, however it is important that you have the mindset to press on!

You cannot wait on someone else to do what you know needs to be done by you. You must conclude **at the earliest time possible** that what needs to be done and what must be done is your responsibility if you desire to achieve optimally while you are here on planet earth—the place of your birth!

Know that Success is in Your Future

Success can still come your way, if you hold your head up despite your pain that you may feel today.

Whether you are facing adversity because of the loss of a loved one, a loss of your job, a medical diagnosis, losing your home, being forced to file bankruptcy, debt mismanagement or any other occurrence, it is important that you know that you can respond appropriately—and you will respond appropriately.

By having the determination to respond favorably to adversity and not giving up or feeling sorry for yourself, you can come up with new and more empowering ways of coming back stronger than you were prior to facing adversity along with achieving far more—if you believe and know that better days lie ahead, and you are committed to bringing those better days into reality by learning and doing what you need to do!

Put in the Required Work that is Needed to Make what You Desire a Reality

You must understand fully that work will be required of you, and you must do what you need to do.

It is important that you realize that the road or journey that you take may not be easy and will require effort by you and you must put a plan in place to do what you need to do. You must have an unrelenting spirit to bring into reality what you desire most after facing adversity and difficult stretches during your life.

You must also realize that adversity can occur on multiple fronts, and it may appear that there is no way out—however you must ask adversity, is that all you have got—as your goal is to always overcome adversity, no matter how daunting the challenge is!

You must be "willing to put in the work" to make what you want or need to happen occur in real time.

Always realize that the adversity that we often face is designed to make us stronger, not weaker in the long run—if you sincerely believe it to be so!

And just **I overcame great adversity** in late 2020 and early 2021 with the transition and burial of the one who brought me into this world, so too must you be prepared to overcome any adversity that you may face now or in the coming years.

You must roar like a lion, even when the prey is scarce, and you must know that better days lie ahead.

Whether you earn six figures or just enough to get by on, you can transform your future to that of lasting success if you have the right approach and you are committed to that approach.

And just as **I** initially began blogging in 2010 in response to an adverse situation where a back injury would not allow me to do the love of my life (jogging) and was not able to jog due to that injury for over a decade—little would I know that those small steps at that time would lead to writing (I had not written an article over 500 words in over 20 years) and the creation of 3 websites, a number of blog sites and a number of books that are helping those who desire lasting wealth building success, attain that success in ways they never imagined!

TheWealthIncreaser.com (a leading blog site for those who desire to achieve wealth in a comprehensive manner) was also created as a result of facing great adversity as the creation of that site was formulated while in delay (2 hour driving delay) during "**snowjam" in 2014** that led to the city of Atlanta and surrounding areas to basically shut down due to inclement weather from a snow/ice-storm—with traffic backed up and cars abandoned for hours and overnight in many areas.

By responding positively to that adverse situation, **TheWealthIncreaser.com** was created as well as a number of other books in the real estate and finance 360 degrees series of books later that year that are helping those who desire exposure to principles and success formulas that are presented in a style that is not the norm, now helping them achieve lasting wealth building success in a comprehensive way do just that.

Always realize that adversity is to be expected, but so too is your future success—if you make the decision to give it your best and you don't rest until you achieve ultimate success.

And even though the pain of losing a loved one may never go away—**so too must you cultivate the mindset of responding positively to adversity in a way that never goes away**—and the knowledge that success at an even higher level must remain steadfast in your mind and heart.

You must stay focused, put a plan in place that you believe in, and know in definite terms that you won't be deterred—regardless of what occurs in your life, locally, nationally or on a <u>worldwide stage</u>—as your present and your future can in large part be written by you, if you do what you need to do!

By responding positively to adversity, you can create what others can't see.

And just as **this book** is written in a style and format that is unorthodox but designed to move you forward in a major way, some may not see the benefit—as they are waiting on book critics, influencers and others to give them the ok—<u>while you are determining for yourself that you can do the management of your finances in a better way—today</u>!

By purchasing <u>any number of books in "The Real Estate & Finance 360 Degrees Series of Books"</u> that can lead you toward success today, or <u>visiting a number of pages on websites that I have created,</u> you can create your own lane or your own avenue that takes you towards success in a more effective and efficient way.

It is imperative that you "respond positively to adversity" and achieve major success from this day forward!

It is important that you attack your finances in a manner where **you are comprehensively in control as the goal**—as by doing so you can achieve much more because you truly know your role.

Your goal is to solve your financial dilemma before you have a financial dilemma where possible!

And just as those around the world who have frequented **TheWealthIncreaser.com** dreamed big and achieved lasting results, so must you also want to <u>dream big</u> and not let others who have a limited dream—put their limitations on you!

You must set boundaries to protect your <u>self-worth</u> and you must know that your self-worth is far more important than your <u>net-worth</u> in the long run.

When you know **you are in control**, you live up to your <u>expectations of yourself</u>—not others expectation of you.

In the remainder of this chapter the importance of <u>controlling the management of your finances</u> so that you can improve upon your finances in "<u>all</u>" areas so that you can manage adversity more effectively will be dived into and discussed at a deeper level.

It is important that you now dig in, and discover new ways to move forward <u>when adversity of a high magnitude </u>occurs!

It is important that you face adversity from the perspective where you can move forward as opposed to going backward, remaining where you are at, or possibly remaining in a depressed state.

You must also realize that adversity can occur on multiple fronts and it may appear that there is no way out—however you must challenge the adversity that you are facing and always have the mindset that you will overcome adversity, no matter how daunting the challenge is as you must be willing to put in the work to make what you want or need to happen occur in real time.

Always realize that the adversity that we face is designed to make us stronger, not weaker in the long run—if you believe it to be so!

You must roar like a lion, even when the prey is scarce, and you must know that better days are definitely ahead when you respond appropriately.

Always remember that you control how you will respond to adverse happenings that will occur throughout your lifetime.

All the best as you respond positively to adversity and achieve major success.

Chapter 2

Character—_You must operate with character at all_
times

It is important that you understand that just because
it appears that an individual has
overwhelming positive qualities and are of high
character—doesn't mean that is the case.

Be sure to do your due diligence as it relates to the
financial professionals and companies that you
conduct business with when utilizing financial
products and services.

If you are "choosing a financial advisor" be sure that
you know the right questions to ask and the right
answers that you should get prior to entering into a
written engagement.

To truly reach your credit and financial goals
successfully—you too must be of high character!

You must be of the highest integrity and character,
regardless of what others are doing!

To move forward at a level that will lead to true
success for yourself and your family you must be of
high character, and you must also make it a point to

associate only with those of high character—
whether it be in your financial or personal
relationships.

Is it any wonder that Bernie Madoff was able to
swindle many out of their finances by having a
pleasing personality and the ability to communicate
financial matters in an effective manner.

**However, if those who invested with Bernie Madoff
had done their "due diligence" and had a <u>real
foundation on how personal finances work</u>—they
would have realized early in the process that having
an advisor manage and have actual control of their
funds—was unsound and impractical at an
elementary financial planning level!**

Another illustration of the quality of character is that
of Barry Minkow (rhymes with kinko)—who
exemplifies charisma and helping others at a high
level—but was also a con man.

Throughout the years he has operated as an
entrepreneur, fraud fighter, pastor, movie actor and
serial swindler. In his lifetime he has shown the best
of character traits and the worst of character traits!

He started out as a kid whiz when he founded ZZZZ Best, a carpet cleaning company that he started from his parent's garage in 1982 at age 16.

The value of the company soared to over $100 million on paper—but it was later determined to be a Ponzi scheme. Minkow was convicted of 57 felonies, sentenced to 25 years, and ordered to pay $26 million in restitution.

After being paroled in 1995 he became a pastor and helped many in the congregation and expanded the membership with his charisma and personality.

He later caused Lennar homes stock to fall drastically by manipulating the stock—in which he pleaded guilty to. In September of 2009 he returned to prison where he was sentenced to serve a 5-year term and a new restitution order of $583 million— the amount Lennar stockholders lost due to manipulation.

It was also determined that Minkow commingled church and personal funds at the church that he pastored. Minkow's greatest gift was that he could inspire others—however he lacked true character in a major way!

While committing the above activities he continued to make excuses and provide reasons for his past behavior.

The point of mentioning Madoff and Minkow as it relates to character is that you must do your due diligence in your credit and financial life, and you must operate at a high level—even when no one is looking.

You must realize that there are many who may not have the charisma of a Madoff or Minkow—but they care a great deal about your future success and operate with a high degree of character!

You must research the company and individual that you choose to represent you in financial matters. Do they have a proven system? Does the system make sense to you?

Do you feel you can really attain success under the system that they promote? Are the returns on investments reasonable?

By asking yourself these and other potent and pertinent questions "prior to" written engagement you can avoid potential problems and better position yourself and your family for future success!

Bad Service & Character

With many companies and individuals an unpleasant experience may be experienced by you at some point. The question then arises as to how effectively the company or individual attempts to correct the unpleasant experience.

Did they try to correct the situation in a sincere manner—or did they leave you <u>feeling less-than satisfied.</u> The answer to that question alone will show you if the company or individual is operating at a high level as far as character is concerned!

Character is a very important quality, and it is something that not only you and those you associate with should strive for but is something that you should look for in all your credit and financial transactions.

It is important that you <u>do your due diligence</u> as it relates to the character of companies and individuals that you choose to represent you or you engage with for business or transactional purposes.

Doing so will help move you and your family forward in your credit and financial life in a more efficient manner!

Whether a company or individual does or does not have a charismatic and inspiring program or approach, you must do your due diligence on the front end and on an ongoing basis, if you want to improve your and your family's credit and finances to a high level and not be taken advantage of unfairly.

If you always "operate at a high level of character" (or at a minimum strive to do so) and "look for high character in others whom you associate with" in all your endeavors, success will be more likely to occur in your and your family's future!

Your character goes a long way in helping you build wealth and achieve your goals!

In a world where wrongdoing and immoral activity seems to abound, it can often be difficult for many to focus and do the right things consistently, whether it be financial or in other areas of their personal affairs.

And with immoral and at times illegal activity happening in what seems to be a constant stream at the local, state and international level—it can often be difficult to operate daily with a **high level of character** on a consistent basis when you are in the process of building wealth.

Even so, it is important that <u>you find the strength</u> to do just that as you embark on your <u>wealth building</u> activities.

It is important that you realize the significance of **being of high character** as it relates to your <u>wealth building efforts</u> and in all other areas of your life.

Character is what you must reflect at all times, even when no one is looking!

As you formulate and put together your <u>wealth building plan</u> you must have the intention of doing so in a <u>responsible manner</u> and in the right manner.

It is important that you develop the right habits that are needed for success on a consistent basis!

Your <u>money management personality</u> will reveal your character to a certain degree. It is also important to operate with<u> balance and with character in all areas of your life</u> so that you can avoid financial strife.

Your integrity must not be compromised even when no one is looking!

It is important that you always have integrity. You <u>don't have to cheat your way through life</u> or engage in unethical or unlawful behavior, regardless of what others around you and/or in higher places do.

By operating with integrity, you will see your goals materialize with more clarity and you will be more likely to achieve the goals that are most important to you.

Your vision of success will be clearer to you, and you will formulate a clearer picture of what you need to do—regardless of the economic climate or the goals that you set because in the end you know that your goals will be met.

Always realize that your path to wealth building success does not have to be compromised.

You can learn how to formulate cash flow statements and put a plan together to improve your cash flow, master your credit and improve in the management of all areas of your finances—and you can operate with a high level of character while doing so.

Always remember that your past failures (and successes) are the building blocks for you to achieve more throughout your lifetime. It is important that you learn from your past failures and not let your past failures affect your current and future success in a <u>detrimental</u> way.

You don't have to approach your future in a <u>fearful manner</u> or let fear and <u>other distractions</u> have the upper hand, if you <u>at this time</u> decide to take a stronger stand!

Final Thoughts on Character

Your ability to <u>operate at all times with integrity</u> will go a long way toward helping you achieve "lasting" wealth building success. Although you may be able to attain short-term success by being of low character and operating illegally or immorally—that is not the best approach for long-term lasting success, whether you are building wealth or trying to achieve anything else.

Always remember that struggle builds character, failure builds character and responding positively to adversity builds character!

And just as it may appear that the author of **Wealth Building NOW** is proactive and has left <u>procrastination</u> in the past (which is largely true), it did not start that way as procrastination occurred on many important tasks. And even though the author of **Wealth Building NOW** has created well over 700 web blog pages—at least several hundred other pages were started and never completed up until this day.

However, by pressing on, learning from past failures and gaining a real commitment to operate daily at a higher level (and with character at all times) procrastination no longer occurred for the most part, and web blog pages were completed from start to finish on a more consistent basis.

As you go through life it will at times appear that those who seem to do wrong prosper the most and those who do right or seem to do right, suffer the most.

Even while witnessing such events, you must remain patient, focused, have faith and have the knowledge and preparation that will allow you to operate daily with character and high standards of excellence as a guiding principle and the season for success for you and your family will come in due time.

You can gain the qualities that you feel you are lacking and pursue other areas of concern by having a yearning to do so and then actually doing so!

It is also important that you operate with freedom of thought and freedom of action in the times that we now live in—regardless of who you are. In a nutshell, <u>thought without the right action</u> is really nothing when you really get down to it.

Therefore, it is important that you do the right thing at all times—even when no one is looking and even when adversity raises its ugly head!

And just as the author of **Wealth Building NOW** operated with patience, focus, knowledge and faith over the years and with character at the forefront (which led to powerful inspiration and direction to create this book in a manner that is totally unique) so too must you operate <u>with those same qualities</u> if you desire to achieve at your highest level of excellence and reach your purpose in your life.

And just as many from around the world are now benefiting in a major way <u>from that inspiration</u>—so too can you create a <u>wealth building future</u> or <u>any future you dream of</u> that can have a real impact on your loved ones, your community and society!

By operating with <u>"character at all times"</u> you can <u>transform your financial position</u> more efficiently and increase your <u>net worth</u> in a more beneficial manner.

Even if others do not have high standards, <u>it is important that you do</u>—as you can move toward lasting success with **more focus**—so that you can achieve what you really want to see come true.

*Always realize that it is **YOU** who needs to do what is necessary to make your dreams come true! And always remember that you can go through life and build wealth without violating the rights of others— and you can make the right moves at the right times that will keep you out of the financial gutters.*

You want to get to a point where you are **operating daily with character** and building wealth with <u>integrity at the core</u> as you open a new door.

Your character goes a long way in helping you build wealth and achieve your goals!

As you formulate and put together your <u>wealth building plan</u> you must have the intention of doing so in a <u>responsible manner</u> and in the right manner.

<u>*It is important that you develop the right habits that are needed for success on a consistent basis!*</u>

Your <u>money management personality</u> will reveal your character to a certain degree and you want to be aware of your money management personality.

It is also important to operate with balance and with character in all areas of your life so that you can avoid financial strife.

Even if others do not have high standards—it is important that you do—as you can move toward lasting success with **more focus** so that you can achieve what you really want to see come true.

Chapter 3

Excellence—_You must have a track record of doing what you need to do at your highest level_

The management of your finances over your lifetime have provided you certain money management skills that you can now use to manage your finances.

Those experiences (whether positive or negative) provide you a base point that you can build off and achieve even more during your lifetime.

You will now learn how you can use your e**X**perience, e**X**pertise and e**X**ercise to achieve at a higher level of e**X**ellence as you build wealth.

Did you know that there are certain factors (known and unknown by many) that can help you achieve more in a more efficient manner?

In this chapter we will analyze how you can use your e**X**perience, e**X**pertise and e**X**ercise to achieve at a higher level of e**X**ellence in the management and improvement of your finances so that you can achieve more as you build wealth.

You can use your financial management skills or lack thereof, to learn new and more forward moving approaches to wealth building.

eXperience

It is important to realize that experience matters for many reasons, not least of which is that only someone who has been through an experience knows the nuances and complexities of dealing with it, and as someone who desires to build wealth more efficiently, your past experiences will help formulate your future success.

Your past actions are done—tomorrow is not here yet; however, you can use your **experience** gained in the past in the management of your finances to your advantage—TODAY!

Look back and **reflect on your life** and see what you did appropriately and where you made mistakes or bad decisions. Use that analysis as a starting point to do more and achieve more during your lifetime.

Always use your past experiences as a building point and never use it to go backward, remain where you are now at, or as an excuse not to do more as you move about throughout your life.

eXpertise

Even though you may not be a financial expert, you do possess an **area of expertise** (or you will eventually get there) that is uniquely your own.

Your **life purpose** or reason for being here on earth at this particular time must be tapped into by you.

There is something inside of you that only you possess!

In your financial life you can achieve more by having the **"mental working knowledge"** that is needed to achieve your financial goals.

You can then get in position to truly pursue your life purpose if you are not doing so at this time.

By properly addressing your finances you can put yourself in position to free up time and not have to worry about your finances so that you can more aggressively pursue your life purpose!

eXercise

You must exercise your **mind, body and soul** on a daily basis and you must take the right actions (exercise what you know for your greater benefit) as it relates to your finances.

Do you know the current state of your finances?

Do you know how to manage your credit effectively throughout your lifetime?

Can you readily identify the areas of your finances that you must address or are those areas a mystery to you?

Do you have an adequate emergency fund or are you unaware of what an adequate emergency fund is?

*I've never ran these and other pressing questions through my mind—**but I now want to—must be your attitude** if you desire to achieve more throughout your lifetime!*

You must run **(exercise in your mind)** these questions through your mind, answer them appropriately and take the right or smart action to get to where you need or desire to be.

By **exercising** those thoughts in your mind and taking corrective action(s) you will be well ahead of most when it comes to the **"effective management of your finances"** throughout your lifetime!

eXellence

By reflecting on your life and your **past experiences** in a sincere manner, utilizing your **current expertise** or the **expertise** that you will later gain and **exercising** what you know **(based in part on the concepts that you are learning in this book)** at your highest level, you will begin to achieve at a higher level of excellence financially as well as in other areas of your life.

You must have a yearning to operate at **"your highest level of excellence"**—even if you are around others who do not have that desire!

You must have a **high standard of excellence** and you must be willing to pursue that higher standard at a level that is the absolute best that is within YOU!

You must operate at your highest level of excellence if you desire to build your wealth more efficiently!

When it comes to **building wealth** it is important that you have a **workable understanding** of what it will take to build wealth to the level that you desire.

It is important that you set lofty goals and you have every intention on reaching those goals. You must "make it a priority" to know the rules of engagement or the rules of the game when it comes to building wealth and you must know how to apply that knowledge effectively throughout your lifetime.

Due to **wealth building** being a broad area—with years of proven strategies for building wealth on and off the books, you have a vast array of choices that can take you to where you need or desire to be.

However, to truly reach your highest potential and achieve at your highest level you must pursue your goals with a high level of excellence!

That means that you must know your cash inflows and outflows on a monthly basis and determine where and if you need to make improvements (get more income/cut expenses or do a combination of the two) and **take action at your highest level of motivation** to do what needs to be done.

You must also make sure that you have an **adequately funded emergency fund** and you know how to **manage credit wisely** during the period in your life where you have a need or plan on utilizing credit.

In addition, you must review your **insurance, investments, taxes, education planning, estate planning/wills and retirement planning** to see if there is room for improvement and then determine the best way to make those improvements based on your current finances.

By doing all of the above you are moving toward building your wealth in a comprehensive way and you are helping to ensure that your goals will be achieved on a more definite day.

You are not leaving your finances to chance, but you are moving toward your goals in a more excellent way because you are systematically approaching your finances and you have a definite timetable for achieving your goals that are measurable.

By pursuing your goals in a **more excellent way** you can put yourself in position to achieve lasting goals and give back or contribute to your favorite causes.

In a world that seems to be take—take—take, you can become a giver.

However, you must do the "in between" or the "behind the scenes" work **at your highest level of excellence** if you desire to achieve more throughout your lifetime and operate at a **higher level of excellence** on a more consistent basis.

Final Thoughts on Excellence

By understanding the role that the **X—FACTORS** play in your life you can put yourself in position to achieve much more during your lifetime.

*Now **is not the time** to protect your comfort zone!*

*Now **is the time to** stretch your mind toward what is truly possible in your life!*

It is important that you <u>establish your credibility of who you really are</u> early by **setting the backdrop** of who you are by "more effectively managing your finances starting today—and throughout your lifetime" so that you can pursue other goals and desires that you may have.

It is also important that you pursue your life purpose or what you were really put on earth to do so that you can **experience** the <u>"joy"</u> that is meant for you.

In addition, you must <u>focus on what is important and meaningful</u> and will really move the needle in your life.

You must not do like those who are busy on a daily basis but don't have the <u>proper focus</u> to achieve what is meaningful and significant.

In most cases they "fall short of reaching their goals" and they often wonder why nothing BIG is happening in their life!

In the end being productive (really achieving what you need or desire to achieve) **is the real measuring stick** as it allows you to do what needs to be done and "move the needle" (achieve meaningful goals) in a manner that takes you to where you need or desire to be.

Achieving the RESULTS that YOU desire or NEED to ACHIEVE must be the measuring point as you pursue excellence!

At this <u>TIME</u> it is critical that you make choices that will significantly move you forward, take initiative on what is important in your life, go after your goals with gusto, push forward like never before—get out of your comfort zone and turn the **X—FACTORS** into known factors in your life!

Use your e**X**pertise to <u>create</u> and put out in the world what is uniquely your own.

Work past your **FEARS** (False Evidence Appearing Real Sometimes) and do more on a daily basis.

The success that you always desired will be in your midst by doing so!

Starting today you must GO!

Exercise "your decision" to do more in your life today!

You and "your family" should have it no other way!

In closing, if you **put your focus on** operating at your highest level of excellence on a consistent basis, things will begin to blossom in your life in ways you never imagined.

Stop for a moment and focus on what you want to achieve throughout your life, determine what you would like to do to help yourself, your family, and others—and make a serious commitment to start on a path to making it happen in real time!

In some cases, you may have to let go in order to grow!

You must always realize that what separates the best from the rest is their daily thoughts and actions and whether they **make the choice** to operate daily at their highest level of excellence, whether consciously or unconsciously.

Isn't it time that you **operate at your highest level** in a way that makes sense!

You too have that same ability to choose—and act!

You no longer must lose—or be a hack!

Starting today you can choose to move forward in a better way!

Starting today you can choose excellence and get momentum to stay!

You and your family should have it no other way!

Excellence—it's inside of you!

Excellence, it's something that you must pursue!

Wealth Building Now has the goal of bringing it all out so that you can make your journey towards building wealth come true!

EXCELLENCE—take what you now have and what you will soon learn and do the **absolute best that you**

can with what you have inside—so that you can experience a smoother ride.

Chapter 4

Imagination—*You must have the ability to dream big and act*

In this day and age, it is often refreshing to see an **original thought or idea.** In this fast-paced world where it seems like everything happens instantly—it can often be difficult for many to come up with an original idea or thought.

The use of **"your imagination"** on a constant basis and in the right manner could lead to increased success for you and your family.

With many of my past successful and very successful clients (an imaginative spirit always seemed to surface) their spirit was always at a high level and enthusiasm—or "fire for life" was paramount!

Many had **ideas and dreams** that on the surface seemed far-fetched—however they believed in their mind that it could be done!

It is important that you have a **big imagination** and you dream big—while you are formulating you credit, finance or real estate goals!

It is "your belief" in "your mind" that gives your **dreams and ideas** the power to actually materialize. If you dream small—or worse yet don't dream at all, you limit the ability of your mind and heart to **make big things happen** in your life.

If you dream big in a limitless and sincere manner and you prepare your mind properly with the <u>right knowledge,</u> you can bring into existence that big dream or idea.

Wealth Building NOW is the result of **dreaming big** and was brought into existence from **inspiration that came from within** and <u>inspiration that was acted upon.</u> **Wealth Building NOW** was also brought into existence by a <u>high level of faith</u> (I knew in a sincere way that success was the only possible outcome) **and imagination!**

By **dreaming big** and taking "consistent" **decisive action** the **mental focus** that was needed along with the **determination** and **personal commitment** that was needed came forth in a powerful manner!

Imagine not listening to naysayers and others who might try to persuade you in the opposite direction of your big dream!

Imagine if readers worldwide could purchase a book and improve their credit, finance and real estate knowledge in a manner that truly served their best interest!

Imagine a book that consumers could go to and actually find what they are looking for—without filler material or other non-relevant information that does not do readers justice as they are pursuing a more excellent way of building wealth!

By **imagining** (dreaming big) that a book could be created that did all the above—**"my imagination"** provided the nucleus to actually bring this and other books into existence along with a number of websites!

You too can make great things happen in your life if you dream big and you pursue your goals <u>in a sincere manner!</u>

You must realize that by **dreaming big** you provide the catalyst for real change that can make a real difference in your life. However, you must realize that it will take <u>preparation on your part</u> if you truly desire to bring your "big dream" into reality!

Wealth Building NOW is in large part the result of "preparation" in the areas of real estate, personal finance, loan processing and daily living that I have done over the past twenty plus years.

By having the preparation that was necessary, **Wealth Building NOW** came into clearer focus in a powerful manner.

You must have the "preparation" that is needed if you desire to bring **your big dream** into reality— whether it be improving your credit and finances to a high level or any other goal **or dream** that you may have in mind!

You must also realize that you must be resilient and diligent and never quit as adversity and other happenings that may cause stress in your life will occur as you move toward your "big dream!"

You must realize that you will have to **"take action"** to make your dream occur! You can't just have faith that it will happen and not actively work **to make it happen.**

However, you must realize that if you stay committed and do the work that is necessary, you can make your **"big dream"** happen!

Whether your goal is to **pursue what you are really passionate about** at your highest level or **improve your credit and finances to a high level** so that you can do what you desire during your lifetime—you can create the environment to make it happen by having a **big imagination** and **dreaming big!**

As far as imagination and your credit and finances go—if you dream big and you sincerely believe that debt payoff or debt pay down will occur in your life and you put a plan in place to actually do so, **you set yourself and your family up for the future success that you desire in all areas of your financial life!**

Always realize that if you don't have an **imaginative spirit**—it can be cultivated over time. Daily meditation along with regular exercise can do wonders for **your imagination** and help you be a better person.

You can improve your focus and get to the point where you want to improve your life in all areas— including your credit and finances.

You can gain the **preparation** that you need—to succeed, by learning and applying the principles and concepts in this book.

By doing so you give **your credit and financial dreams** a real chance to materialize because you will have the preparation that is necessary (on the front end) to make your dream(s) materialize!

By focusing on what is important and gaining the **preparation that is needed** you can move forward in an effective manner and you will increase your **imaginative thoughts** (you start to dream big) and you will start to believe that you can **attain goals** that you never thought possible.

If you "focus in" at the right time in your life **you can accomplish many goals that you may have thought were out of reach for you and your family.**

Can you imagine yourself not owing anyone?

Of course, you can!

The key is that you must get started today—so that things can begin to go your way!

Reading **Wealth Building NOW**

Will show you how!

The actual application will be up to you!

However, you will know what you need to do!

Get started today—on a financial journey that can move you and your family forward—in a major way!

Use **your imagination to dream big** and follow your dream with a <u>written plan</u> to make it happen. Be sure to use **goal setting** along with <u>proven systems </u>to make your and your family's dream a reality—starting today!

<u>You now know that "preparation" is a key component for reaching the success that you desire!</u>

Always remember that when you are in the process of improving your credit and finances **you must dream big!**

You must also use your **imaginative** <u>thoughts</u> in a manner that serves your and your family's best interest!

And always remember that there are no limits on what you can do, if you don't set any limits!

If you set limits, you not only limit what you can do, you put in motion the mental processes to not make your dreams come true!

Now is the time that you unleash the creative energy that you have inside of you to do great things in your life—whether it be with your credit or finances or any other area of your life!

Wealth Building NOW will help you do just that in the most efficient and effective manner possible if you apply the principles properly to your unique financial position and align those principles with your goals!

Isn't your future worth utilizing your time in a manner that will really benefit you and your family, so you can achieve a lifetime of success that can change your future in a meaningful and significant way—starting today!

It is important that **you use your imagination** while you are in the process of **building your wealth** or achieving many other goals that you may desire.

You must use the inspiration that you receive to see what you desire or see the direction that you should go. By using your mind, heart, and mental faculties to **imagine that what you desire** has already occurred, you put yourself on a serious path toward success!

However, you must realize that is only the starting point! Real work will be required of you on a consistent basis to **make what you imagine come to realization** in real time!

Just as I decided to create this book using my imagination so that you and others could achieve financial and wealth building success in a comprehensive manner—and then followed through on that big dream by putting in the required work (effort) to **create this book**—so too must you apply yourself on a consistent basis to make what you desire a reality in the area of your choosing or in the area of your life purpose.

You must **use your imagination** to dream big and follow through with action and not pay attention to naysayers or others who may try to talk you out (negative energy) of your **big dream.**

In the area of personal finance and wealth building you must give deeper, more meaningful thought about your finances and your financial future—and what you can achieve in your financial future.

A vivid **active imagination** on a consistent basis is the key to your success. Using your **imagination** effectively to build wealth is not taking your mind to fantasy land—quite the contrary, it is formulating a picture in your mind of something that "you believe" your heart and mind can make real and can be of significant benefit to you, your family, and others.

You must have a **"financial mindset of resiliency"** and gain the mental toughness along with the "know how" of how to manage your finances effectively for the rest of your life.

Imagination in lay terms is using the power that you have within to make something big happen in your future and then using the energy from that power to form a mental image of something (what you **sincerely desire** to occur in your future) to more effectively help guide you to bring into reality what you imagined.

What you imagine normally won't happen in a moment but is a process! It may not appear real at this moment to you and others, however within your heart and mind you see it as real, and you know that you are truly willing to put in the work to "make it real."

Even though it is not real or present at this time, you know that you are determined to use your creativity (a major part of your imagination) to bring into existence that which you imagined!

It is important that you realize that "accidental accomplishment" of major goals rarely occur. You need to have **clear vision** so that you can **stay on course** and go after your goal(s) **in a passionate** and intentional manner!

If you don't have a clear picture or vision of the goals in front of you that were formed by **your imagination**—you "lessen the passion" that you have inside to accomplish what **you imagine** in a more effective and efficient manner.

Will you choose to blow with the wind (go to a place that is not for you) or will you choose a proven and definite path to success?

What is your real desire for your life? Do you have definite goals that you will sincerely pursue? What is your compass and what is directing your life at this time?

What is guiding your vision of your future?

Better yet, who is guiding and shaping your vision of your future?

It is imperative that you use **your imagination** along with **sound planning** to reach your goals more efficiently.

You must see your goals on the inside first—so they can take place on the outside later! Don't choose the easiest route, as it is often grounded in many pitfalls! You won't ever quit if you have **clear vision!**

Have you lost your view of your future and what you can really do?

Do you even have a vision?

Do you even desire to have a vision?

Once you get immersed into **pursuing you purpose** and using **your imagination** in the right way you will begin to achieve "beyond your imagination."

You can put yourself in position to **learn what needs to be learned** to achieve at a higher level on a daily basis in your wealth building effort by having a sincere desire to do so.

You can put yourself in position to use **your imagination** in more effective ways on a more consistent basis.

You can use **your imagination** and **Wealth Building NOW** to get your financial future right—so that you can later say—**WOW!**

Wealth Building NOW serves as your springboard to wealth building success if you are now willing to give it your absolute best!

And always be open to **imagining or re-imagining** a brighter future with something you already use—your mind and heart.

And always be open to using your heart and mind for **wealth building**—now is the time for your fresh start.

Imagine the possibilities for your future in a more inspiring way.

Imagine achieving all that you desire—starting today.

Imagine, Re-imagine—but most important of all—ACHIEVE WHAT YOU SET OUT TO ACHIEVE AS YOU ARE THE ONE WHO MUST TRULY BELIEVE!

Chapter 5

Focus—You must zoom in and pursue what you desire with laser like focus

It is important that you understand that **properly focusing helps you attain your goals in a more efficient and effective manner** and helps you see your future from the right perspective by blocking out all negative interference that you may have in your life, so that you can achieve more.

Proper preparation on your part will go a long way in giving you the "proper focus" that is needed for your and your family's future credit and finance success.

By comprehending this chapter at your highest level, you can learn how to improve your focus daily so that you can attain the goals that will serve your and your family's best long-term interests!

If you see your credit and financial future clearly and you **focus on what is truly important** by utilizing the empowering credit and finance information in this book, you can reach your goals and objectives in not only an effective manner but also a more efficient manner.

Proper focus allows you to concentrate on what is truly important and will take you and your family to where you need or want to be!

If your goal is to manage and improve your credit and finances to a high level, you can do so if you have the **right focus.**

Having the right focus means concentrating on your future goals and objectives with laser like precision.

By having the know-how of what you need to do and actually knowing how you can improve your credit and finances to a high level you can put yourself in position for major success in your and your family's future.

If you use your know-how, proper execution and **proper focus—all working in conjunction**, you make your and your family's future success much more likely to occur.

It is also important that you include written goal setting as part of your focusing efforts if you truly want to reach your and your family's future goals.

Focusing allows you to make room in your mind to put what you really want to "achieve" at the forefront of <u>your mental thought process</u> on a daily basis.

"Proper focus" requires that you <u>block out all negative distractions in your life</u> and not let the opinions of others deter you from reaching your goals.

*Did you know that there are **basically 3 ways** that you can approach occurrences that will happen in your life or that may happen around you?*

1) there are things in life that you absolutely cannot change

2) there are things in life that you could possibly change—but you are often reluctant to do so for varying reasons

3) there are things that are **totally under your control,** and **you have the power** to do something about in a meaningful and significant way—today

The **3rd option**—mentioned above is what this book focuses on, and it is what you too should spend your energy **focusing on** if you desire to maximize your future success!

You must focus on things that you can do something about RIGHT NOW—at this time!

By "consciously or unconsciously" focusing on the **1st or 2nd option** by complaining, <u>making excuses</u> and <u>otherwise letting distractions rule over you</u> on a consistent basis, you are displaying a lack of understanding of how to truly transform your future.

And by doing so you are **taking your focus** in a direction that does not best serve your long-term interests!

Because you can't or often won't do anything about what you can't change—or possibly change you are wasting time and <u>mental energy</u> that you could be using to focus on things that you can change and things that you absolutely have the power to change!

By **properly focusing** and using <u>written goals</u> you give your mind <u>even more clarity</u> and <u>your daily mindset will be improved</u> because you will know with certainty that **if you focus** and do what you put in writing, <u>your future goals will be attained!</u>

Don't let your dreams, thoughts, ideas, theories, and goals die inside of your mind! Put them in

writing and then <u>take action</u> and "properly focus" to make what you desire a reality!

Did you know that some of your most powerful thoughts and ideas (inside your mind) will float away and possibly never return if you don't put them in writing or record your thoughts and ideas in some other manner?

By putting your thoughts, ideas and goals in writing you can **improve your focus** and reach your and your family's <u>credit, financial, and life goals </u>in a more efficient manner!

Proper Focus means that you are paying attention to your future goals at such a high level that you see your success clearly and you know in your mind and heart that you will not be distracted along the way!

You know with a **high level of certainty** that you are <u>"truly serious" </u>and **you intend on reaching your future goals in an efficient and effective manner!**

Proper focus is a <u>quality</u> that you must have if you desire to attain your goals and objectives in an efficient manner.

If you sincerely want success for yourself and your family, you must **focus on reaching your goals** at your highest level of thought.

Doing so will put you on a path to true success!

Once you **focus** and attain your goals on a consistent basis, you will put yourself in position to enjoy your life on your terms.

You will no longer be at a disadvantage in your credit, financial, and other areas of your life.

You must have a yearning, passion and true desire to reach your goals—whatever they may be!

If you are "properly focused" and you have a "true desire" to reach your credit and financial goals— others will feel and see your enthusiasm and your future success will be more likely to occur.

Likewise, if you are not properly focused and you are not truly determined to reach your credit and financial goals—your future success will be less likely to occur and others will feel your lack of enthusiasm.

It is important that you focus your thoughts on what you desire, and likewise—you must desire what you focus on!

There is no reason why you should focus on (waste energy)—whether consciously or unconsciously, things that you can't do anything about or things that you won't do anything about—if you desire to attain success in a more effective and efficient manner!

Always remember that to be highly successful, you must "properly focus" and you must have "passion" in whatever you do! You must not pursue your goals in a half-hearted manner if you desire to achieve at your highest level!

Use the knowledge that you have learned in this chapter to your and your family's best advantage!

Proper preparation and **proper focus** along with a <u>burning desire to succeed on the inside</u>—along with a <u>high level of determination</u> will take your success to a high level.

Do you have "staying power" when things get tough?

You already know that the way that you "look at life" and how you <u>respond to adversity is the key to your and your family's future success!</u>

You must be "unstoppable" in your journey toward reaching your goals and objectives!

No obstacle or adversity that you encounter should detour (or deter) you from reaching your and your family's future credit and financial goals!

You must always focus on what you want to bring into existence, and you must bring into existence that which you want—by properly focusing on what you desire!

You cannot merely talk about what you desire, think about what you desire or dream about what you desire! You must **focus** and take consistent action and make what you desire—a reality!

When you really get down to it, execution is all that really counts!

You must also find out what you are passionate about and what your true calling or gift in your life really is!

You must not do like many who live their life inappropriately and when they reach their golden years they look back in regret after knowing that they had the gift to do more.

You must realize that you now have the potential to achieve many of your credit and financial goals by

reading this book—however, "potential to do so" is really nothing in the grand scheme of things!

Until you sincerely <u>decide to put into action</u> that which can really benefit you and your family on a consistent basis, <u>potential serves no real purpose!</u>

You can change the patterns of your past and do more in your life! You can change your future for the better in a major way—starting today!

Wealth Building NOW provides you a <u>"real opportunity"</u> to **re-calibrate your mind** and provides you the opportunity to master the **mental working knowledge** that you need to succeed—**BIG TIME!**

What do you really desire at this time?

You must now find out what you really desire in your future, **properly focus** and <u>properly prepare your mind and heart</u> to <u>make it happen!</u>

You now have a clearer understanding of what **you need to do** and **focus on** to make "what you desire" a reality—<u>now</u> go do it!

Goal setting and **properly focusing** require a concerted effort on your part, and it all starts inside your mind and heart.

The wrong actions of others should not bother you as much as the wrong actions that "you" take or the mistakes that you make! You control your future, and you decide the amount of **focus, commitment, and effort** that you will exert daily.

You must pursue your goals with **zeal,** and you must **pay attention** or **focus on** what is important in your future! What is motivating you to currently give it your absolute best? You can utilize "attentive focus" to "stretch your mind" and achieve more by setting significant goals and doing your best in terms of **focus, commitment, and effort** to reach the goals that you desire most.

By formulating those goals that are most important to you and seeing them already accomplished and putting in the required effort, the atmosphere for them to materialize can be created—and the actual focus and action will lead to the goals being achieved by you.

It is imperative that you realize that nothing major occurs until you leave excuses behind and properly focus and act on what you want to see become real!

Even though **Wealth Building NOW** is a book that is designed to inspire and encourage you to do more in your life—the **focus, commitment and effort** that is needed for you to achieve your goals **MUST** come from inside of you.

*Let's now discuss in greater detail how you can improve the **focus commitment and effort** in your life and achieve the goals that you desire more efficiently.*

Don't continue to hinder what you can accomplish by setting limits within your mind!

You must not let your past circumstances (or current circumstances) put out the light and dim your dreams! You must **AIM high** in spite of where your mind and heart currently resides—and reload and fire again in spite of failure or less than desirable outcomes.

Success must be your barometer and guiding principle in your life and you must not let anything— or anyone deter you from **moving to action** in a manner that takes you toward the success that you desire.

Something big and beyond what you think you can do lies in the horizon!

Don't lose that vision that you have inside of you to do something big during your lifetime.

Determine right now to set major goals and make the decision to never quit until you achieve them by properly focusing. Your hope and vision of your future must be made real by you by visualizing it— and taking real steps (**focus, commitment and effort**) toward truly achieving your vision!

You want to have focus, and a vision of what you want to accomplish. Action is responding appropriately to what you see and the more focused you are, the more likely you are to take the right action and accomplish your goals.

Actuality or realization is experiencing in real time what you hoped for, planned for, worked hard for, and properly focused on and visualized—using faith as a guide to take you there!

Now is the time and season in your life that you unleash the force that is within you to give your hopes and vision a real chance to materialize in your life by moving to action on a consistent basis from this day forward with increased focus as your guiding light.

If you get an **"active mindset"** and not follow the crowd, you can do more in a day than many do in a week—not because you are so great but because you "put in motion a plan within your mind" to take consistent action—and you followed through on that plan in a sincere, focused and determined manner.

If you lack the ability or desire at this time to act, you can develop the ability to take consistent action if you sincerely desire to do so. However, the decision to do so must start inside of you—and it is your participation that will make your goals and dreams come true.

It is important that you realize that the life that you live can be improved significantly if you make a sincere and determined effort at this time to raise the bar and pursue your goals with **more focus** on a daily basis.

There really is no stopping a mind that is made up and that is properly **focused, committed, and willing to put in the required effort** consistently.

What is **your motive** for going after what you truly desire to achieve in a more **focused** manner? Challenge yourself to utilize your mind, body, and soul at a higher level—daily—right now!

If you take the **first step** you will find out that the power to do what needs to be done is already within you—just waiting for you to make a sincere and focused effort at achieving what you desire.

Pursuing your goals in the right manner will not cause you to feel miserable no matter how adverse your situation is because you will see your goals clearly and know that the outcomes that you desire will occur.

Always realize that you can't correct that which you are unable or unwilling to confront! What you may now feel is impossible, is possible if you allow your mind to dwell in an environment where all things are possible.

Just as **Wealth Building NOW** and the success of this book at inception was brought into existence by having the **focus, commitment and effort** that was required on a consistent basis that was necessary to make this book a success—you too can do the same with your dreams and vision—in your area of choice!

How you see your current situation and future success is critical!

If you can't see the other side of the mountain (your future situation) you must get a better view by rising (flying over) and looking over the mountain—then you will see the other side and know how to get there much more efficiently.

Likewise, if you get a better view—and you can see or visualize a better path to your future financial success—you can also get there more efficiently!

Change your position, change your view, and change your future by approaching your future in a more **intelligent, consistent, and proactive manner—** whether it be with your building of wealth or any other area of your life.

The way that you are looking at your current finances may be from a **limited view** because you don't have a **comprehensive or more focused approach** where you can see over the mountain and **"know"** the best way to go over around or through it.

By changing your view, you will be on your way to getting the outcomes that you desire on a more consistent basis.

You can get a full view of the mountain, forest, rivers, and anything else that may be obstructing your view (future).

If you get a full view (comprehensive picture) of your finances—you will not only see your positive outcomes in a more focused way, but you will work even harder to bring those outcomes into existence because <u>you will take the right actions to get momentum rolling</u> to actually make what you desire materialize more efficiently.

Wealth Building NOW is designed to create excitement, movement and provide you a way of **focusing on your future** in a manner that will allow you to achieve your dreams more effectively.

In the end realize that there is a lot that you can do to improve your credit and finances. Also realize that there is a lot that can keep you where you are now at if you fail to focus properly and take the right action!

Are you trying to rationalize your inaction currently or are you ready for a challenging but more rewarding future?

What have you done for not only yourself but others as well? In the end, it is how you affected others on planet earth that really counts!

Be sure to set some **meaningful and significant goals** today and go after them with all of the gusto that you can muster up inside.

The success that you desire will take you higher if you visualize your future and put in the **focus, commitment and effort** that is required!

Wealth Building NOW provides you the nucleus (opportunity) to take action and start on a path toward achieving your dreams more efficiently, whether by the effective use of this book or any other method that you feel is appropriate.

Now is the time that you not only hope for successful outcomes, but now is the time that you believe in yourself like never before and know deep within that without a doubt something good is going to happen in your life daily because you are in control, and you know what you need to focus on.

Decide right now to start on a path of living with joy on the inside, living with high spirits on the inside and feeling good about your future on the inside— and the outside—as you are now on a smoother glide.

By doing so your journey to success will be a much smoother ride!

In closing, **5 steps that you can take NOW** to improve your focus and reach financial success in a timelier manner will be presented.

It is important that you realize that regardless of where you are now at, there are times in your life that "you will lose focus" and you must then get back on track.

You can **re-focus your mind for success** or adjust your mind and daily habits to achieve more in your life.

You possess the ability to achieve at a much higher level daily and it all starts with using your mind and heart in more engaging and creative ways!

As it relates to your wealth building efforts, you can re-focus by becoming more conscious of your actions in the following areas:

1) Being more Aware of your financial outlook

2) Being more Mature about your finances

3) Having a Secure outlook about your future

4) Being of high Character at all times

5) Having an Action mindset daily

Re-focusing Your Mind for Success by Increasing Your Financial Awareness

- Awareness

You must be aware of what is going on and occurring in your financial life on a consistent basis. You must take a "big picture" view of what is occurring in your financial life, and it does not have to be made difficult if you have the right approach. Are you AWARE of your monthly income and expenses?

Do you know your annual income, and do you know your outstanding debt? Do you know your net worth?

Do you know how to manage your credit effectively at this time?

Do you know all the areas of your finances that you NEED to address or is it difficult for you to put them all together at this time in a logical manner in your mind?

You must have a highly effective mental system that you can carry within your mind that allows you to do all the above on the front end—if you desire to maximize your future success!

Even if you do know all the areas (most people don't)—just knowing is not enough—you must have a systematic approach for improving in all the above-mentioned areas in a manner that will give you the results that you desire or the results that you need to achieve.

Not being aware of any or all the above could be adding unneeded stress and anxiety to your life that you could be living without. If only you were AWARE of what you needed to know as it relates to your personal finances, and you had an efficient manner for managing what you were aware of—you could "significantly reduce" the stress in your life.

Re-focusing Your Mind for Success by Being More Financially Mature

- Maturity

You must take a MATURE approach to managing your finances and not do like many consumers do.

Many consumers do not have a good financial foundation and many have no clue about how they manage their finances or how they will achieve their financial goals and objectives.

Do you practice solid habits daily with your finances or are you easily distracted and go off on the opposite path of where you intended to go? If you go in the opposite direction of your future goals on a number of occasions, you may lack the financial maturity that is needed to achieve major success!

Re-focusing Your Mind for Success by Being More Secure About Your Financial Future

- Secure

You must never be insecure as you move toward reaching your future financial goals. You must feel **worthy of the success** that you are pursuing, and you must feel comfortable about your path to success. You must **see your future success clearly** and you must feel worthy of achieving what you see. You must always love, honor, and believe in yourself— because if you don't, why should others?

Re-focusing Your Mind for Success by Being of High Character as You Manage Your Financial Affairs

- Character

You must be of the highest character and always strive to do the best that is within you in the right manner.

Regardless of what others may be doing you must do your absolute best regardless of who is or is not looking.

It is important that you have high standards, and you associate with those who are of high character—and you must make it a habit to seek and engage with those who are of high character daily.

Re-focusing Your Mind for Success by Having an Action Mindset as You Manage Your Financial Affairs

- Action Mindset

You must make it a habit to act immediately on matters of real significance and importance as it relates to your finances.

By doing so you can put yourself in position to create something new, solve problems for yourself, your family—and humanity!

You can be a blessing to yourself, your family, and others if you take the right ACTION on a consistent basis.

Do you at this time desire to get started on a serious path to success?

You can NOW do so—by giving it your absolute best!

Final Thoughts on Focusing

You can develop the right habits that are needed for consistent success if you have the determination and commitment level that is needed to "focus" or "re-focus your mind" on what is important to your future success.

You must have a "heightened awareness" as it relates to your finances and not be like others that you may be around who are only "going through the motions" and are not AWARE of what is "really" going on around them in their financial life.

You don't have to live monthly with uncertainty about what you can and can't do!

You don't have to <u>mismanage your credit </u>and pay creditors huge amounts of interest while you sit by and earn paltry returns.

You don't have to have a "confused mind" about how to address all areas of your finances in an appropriate manner.

You must approach your finances in a more intelligent, consistent, and proactive manner (a more

MATURE manner) if you desire to achieve at a high level and truly reach the goals that you desire.

You must have a SECURE outlook about your future, and you must get a feeling on the inside of you that says in a sincere way—I CAN DO THIS, and I WILL DO THIS!

As you pursue your goals you must always be of high CHARACTER, and you must know that by pursuing your goals in a righteous manner—you can achieve more—and you can do more during your lifetime!

You must have an ACTIVE MINDSET as by having one you can do more and achieve more. Whether you now know it or not—you have the ability to achieve much more on a daily basis and it all starts with you thinking that you can do more—putting a plan in place to do more—and then actually doing more by taking action.

The active use of your mind will allow you to "re-focus on what you need to focus on" at a higher level of thought and will take you towards the future goals that you desire for yourself and your family at a much faster pace than if you did not do so.

You must from this point forward realize that it is "your responsibility" to be **aware of** what needs to be done in your financial life.

Even if you are immature in other areas of your life—now is the time to approach your finances in a **mature** manner.

You are responsible for **securing** a prosperous future for yourself and your family and you must be of high **character** as you take that journey. You are responsible for gaining the right habits that can help you get to where you need or want to go in an efficient manner.

You must develop a mindset to take the right **action** when it is in your best interest to do so! You must do so in an intense and immediate fashion and really put your heart into it if you desire to achieve at your highest level.

You must realize that it is your responsibility to bring into existence a new reality for yourself and your family—and you must fully understand that no one can do it but you and that is as it should be if you are sincere in making your dreams come true!

You must understand that even though there have been many overnight sensations—success is far more likely for those who operate on a consistent basis over a period, and many achieve great results by doing so—and you can do the same if you take the right action consistently!

You have the power within to "focus" or "re-focus your energy" on what is important in your financial life and attain the goals that can put you in control of your financial future—and keep you in control— starting today!

You can do so by consistently applying the principles in this book and pursuing other areas of wealth building knowledge in other ways!

Wealth Building NOW desires that you have a prosperous and productive future where you focus on your finances in a comprehensive manner and by using the focusing tips in this chapter and implementing the **5 steps** mentioned above in your life in an intelligent, consistent, and proactive manner—you can start or continue a path to ensuring that you will do just that.

Chapter 6

Confidence—_You must know within your mind and heart that you desire to set yourself apart_

It is important that you have a high level of **"confidence"** and a positive outlook about your and your family's wealth building future in these difficult times that we now live in.

As economies around the world continue to transition, it is important that you understand the importance of **having confidence in yourself** as you move forward in any economic environment.

It is imperative that you have a view of your future that is prosperous and will get you the results that you desire, regardless of how the current and future economy will affect others!

You have all that you need inside of you to make your future a successful one if you believe you can do it.

Don't let the way others view and see the current economy or future economic environments be a deterrent to you successfully transforming your future in a major way.

However, you must realize, **it takes more than just confidence** to transform your wealth building future! You must also have the <u>financial means and a detailed plan</u> (or the determination to get to that point) that will take you to where you need, or want to be.

By having **"confidence"** in your future you send a consistent signal to your mind and heart that you will be successful and accomplish your goals—even if others don't!

By having a **high level of confidence** about your financial future it will help you cultivate habits that are good for you and your family. You must not fear the future no matter how uncertain it may appear.

You must always love, honor, and believe in yourself and by demonstrating a high level of **"confidence"** in your future, you are doing just that.

If you currently lack **confidence,** you can increase your **confidence level** by using written goals and believing in yourself, your family, and your future so strongly that defeat is never an option!

If you currently have **confidence** in your future—you still need a <u>written plan for achieving your future</u>

goals, a high level of determination, the ability to overcome adversity and difficult stretches during your life that you may face in the future, a high degree of commitment and the self-discipline to carry out the goals that you outline in your written plan.

You must have a heart-felt desire to make your future a prosperous and successful one!

If you have **confidence** in your future goals you will not half-heartedly pursue your future goals.

You must pursue your future goals whole-heartedly and with the passion of the real expectation that your future goals will be successfully reached.

Your vision of your future success must be so clear to you that you believe that your success has already occurred!

Many who don't reach their financial or other goals do so because they lacked the confidence in their mind to really believe that it could and would happen.

Don't let that be you!

You must understand that if you don't "really" believe that a successful and prosperous future will happen—it won't happen.

Having a high level of confidence means your "spirit of success" should embody everything that you do, if you truly want to make your dreams come true!

You must realize fully that you are the determining factor, and you control your future!

Use that knowledge to move yourself and your family towards your future goals!

Whether your future goals are to improve your credit, save for that great family vacation that you always wanted to take, reaching your retirement goals, funding your children's college education <u>or any other goals or objectives that you may have, you are the determining factor that will make what you are pursuing occur.</u>

Again, it is imperative that you have **"confidence in your future"** if you truly want to move yourself and your family forward in a major way!

As we move along in this millennium, many are attempting to make a serious turn in the <u>direction in</u>

their life, and achieve lasting success in the management of their credit and finances is high on their list.

As you turn in the direction of making your life more prosperous, you must realize that a key component to achieving the wealth building success that you desire is how you look at your past, present and future.

And it is more important than ever that **you have confidence in your future** regardless of the political and economic climate that you find yourself in.

You must clearly understand the importance of why you must have confidence in your future and know the steps that you can take to bring more confidence into your life!

It is important that you see success in all areas of your life and particularly in the area of your credit and finances!

You must want (in your heart and mind) to see how you can use personal financial statements to your advantage, know how you can master your credit effectively and know how you can address all of the important areas of your finances in a way that will take you to where you want or need to be.

You can increase your confidence about your future by learning how to use personal financial statements to your advantage.

It is beneficial for you to have the knowledge of how you can use **personal financial statements** for the greater benefit of yourself and your family.

By knowing your monthly income and the monthly outflow of cash **(cash flow)** that you utilize to pay your monthly expenses you can get a clearer picture of how you manage your finances now—and how you can make improvements, thus improving your confidence in general and particularly about how you can manage your finances better.

In addition, you want to see how your **yearly income** and **yearly outflow of cash** that you utilize to pay your yearly expenses affect your household.

A **personal income statement** will help you see just that and will also provide you an even clearer picture of your overall finances and where you can possibly go in your future.

In addition you want to take a serious look at your **assets** and your **liabilities** so that you can determine your **net worth** and a **balance sheet** will assist you in this process.

Your net worth is a key metric that can be used at the various stages of your life to help you see how you are doing financially!

By learning how to use personal finance statements to your advantage, you are showing a <u>real commitment</u> to improve your financial condition and the success or goals that you desire to occur will be made more realistic for you if you utilize the knowledge gained from those statements in the right way.

You will put yourself in position to operate daily with more **confidence and optimism** and a <u>feeling of joy</u> can live inside of your heart and mind on a continuous basis.

You can increase your confidence about your future by learning how you can master your credit effectively to your advantage.

It is important that you have working knowledge of how you manage your credit and how you can manage your credit more effectively. You must have a **"meaningful understanding"** of how credit works and you must have working knowledge of the "5 credit factors" so that you can apply that knowledge throughout your lifetime.

By keeping your **"payment history positive"** and your **"utilization rate"** or the amount of your available credit that you use below 10% you will be on a good path toward credit management.

You must also manage your credit effectively **"over time"** and you must have several **"types"** of credit (your credit mix) and seek new credit sparingly to keep your **"hard inquiries"** at an acceptable level if you desire to maximize your credit and credit score throughout your lifetime or during the period in your life that you desire to utilize credit for major transactions.

You can increase your confidence about your future by addressing all the important areas of your finances.

It is important that you know what you must address financially, and you must use that knowledge to actually **manage the major areas of your finances in a comprehensive manner** and in a manner that is more beneficial for you and your family.

You must ensure that your **insurance coverage** (no pun intended) in all areas that can benefit you has at least been looked at and analyzed—and where appropriate improved upon or added to your insurance profile. You must **invest** both inside and outside of your **retirement accounts** so that you can achieve the goals that you desire.

You must minimize or avoid the **taxes** that you pay in as effective a legal manner as possible. You must establish an **emergency fund** that is appropriate for you and your family.

You must establish an **education plan** for your children, if necessary, at the earliest time possible, and finally you must complete your **estate plan/will(s)** in a timely manner as well.

Final Thoughts on Confidence

Your determination to look at your finances in a proactive manner can lead to you gaining "added confidence" in the way that you look at and respond to financial occurrences at this time and throughout your lifetime. There is no reason that you should **fear** your financial future or let **distractions** that occur during your lifetime rule the day.

Now is the time that you use your "new found or newly created confidence" as it relates to your finances to **worry less, let go of anxiety, leave fear and frustration in your past, put forth more effort, and leave all excuses** behind.

By using personal financial statements, mastering your credit, and improving your finances in all areas —you can **confidently** look at your future and pursue the success that you desire in a more definite way.

You can then pursue other goals or your life purpose in a manner that is empowering and can really take you to where you need or desire to be.

It is important that you understand what is best for your long-term financial health and you must organize your thoughts with awareness of where you want to go, and you must have a steady confidence as you move toward where you want to go!

It is you who must organize your thoughts and find the best route to long-term success based on your goals and dreams!

Even if you are on a prosperous path toward financial success you must still pursue your goals with passion and always know that adversity or unwanted happenings will occur during your life.

It is you who must find a way (possibly with the assistance of others) to come through your adversity and recognize that you are now stronger and you can achieve more.

You must realize that adversity has occurred and you can grow from it if you believe you can, and you take steps to make the growth happen by taking the appropriate action.

You must gain or regain your confidence and move forward!

You must be "proactive" (notice the emphasis on proactive), formulate and execute your goals in a manner where you have the right frame of mind (cultivate success qualities to a higher level in your life) as you build wealth.

*You must have confidence in your ability to improve your personal finances and build wealth efficiently in any economic environment and in **Appendix B and the BONUS SECTION** you will learn what you can do to gain even more clarity and focus toward success as you manage your finances.*

As the world turns and happenings that defy logic occurring in a rapid fire manner on a regular basis, it can often be difficult to **see your future with clarity** and **have the confidence** that you will make your **wealth building** and other dreams come true.

By having confidence in your future you can provide your mind and heart the inspiration, determination and <u>imagination</u> to <u>avoid procrastination</u> and <u>reach your destination</u> so that you can respond appropriately to any financial situation.

OK, now that you feel somewhat confident about your future, let us now **explore in 3 steps** why you must have **even more confidence in yourself** and **confidence in the financial success** that lies in front of you, if you do what you need to do.

- **You must know that you have a financial management system in place that will allow your mind to grow**

It is important that you approach the management of your finances with <u>a system of management</u> that is familiar to you, makes sense to you and can practically be put into effect by you—so that you can start on a journey toward <u>sincerely making</u> your dreams come true.

You must have a "made up mind" that **now is the time** that you dig in and pursue what you need to do to see your way through <u>regardless of any adversity</u> that you are now facing, have faced in your past or might face in your future.

By doing so you put your mind in position to really "<u>tune in</u>" to what is truly important and significant—

and you open up the possibility of unlimited growth by expanding the possibilities of what you can achieve throughout your lifetime.

- **You must use the best system around that works best for you as you move forward toward making your dreams come true**

It is important that you search out and find <u>the best comprehensive financial management system</u> that works the best for you.

Whether you find <u>this book</u> or other books in "The Real Estate & Finance 360 Degrees Series of Books" to be the most appropriate for you, some other website(s), books, financial planners and other professionals—or a culmination of a number of sources—it is **your responsibility** to find what works best for you and your family.

By having a **yearning and determination** to search out the best sources of financial information that will provide you the best financial or wealth building foundation—you set yourself up for building wealth more effectively and efficiently at the <u>various stages</u> in your life!

- **You must "put into action" your approach so that it is beyond reproach (you must actively**

address your finances in a comprehensive manner)

It is you who **must take decisive action** and create a cash flow statement at a minimum, **manage your credit and finances optimally** and put into motion the effective management of your insurance planning, investment planning, tax planning, emergency fund planning, education planning, estate/wills planning and retirement planning throughout your lifetime.

Just learning **what is in this book** (or any highly effective wealth building book) and not putting what you have learned into motion will not take you to where you need or desire to be.

By putting into action the needed steps and determining what you desire to occur in your future in a real way—you are displaying **confidence in yourself** and your financial future.

Regardless of what others are doing or how they look at their future financially and otherwise, you must operate daily with a **high level of confidence** and really **have a feel for your future** and a **real handle** on your future.

You must not only shoot for the moon or stars, you must also raise the bars and have confidence that you will reach mars (a new dimension where you need or desire to be)!

You must have the urgency to **act now** so that you can avoid or reduce the likelihood of adversity or an emergency disrupting your life in a significant way.

Your decision to change is predicated on the pain of now (how you feel at this time) being more painful than what you desire to feel in your future—thereby forcing your heart and mind to take the steps that you need to take at a very high level at this time so that you can operate at a level of confidence that is unmatched by anything that you have ever experienced in your life!

By applying what you have learned in this chapter on a **consistent basis** you put yourself in position to **win the majority** of your races.

You must have confidence in your future and what lies ahead even when the vision appears murky or even when life happenings go in the opposite direction of what you expected!

Even though you may start out at a certain level and not truly believe—if you take steps to move forward and work toward what you conceive—you can reach higher than you expected and exponentially reach more success than you ever thought you would achieve!

Your goal is to have confidence about what lies ahead even though the vision that you have may not be totally clear at this time.

You too must get started on your path to giving it your best and accept nothing less than continuous success, and it begins in a big way by **having confidence** that the goals that you seek, will materialize!

You must at all times **feel worthy of the success** that you are **about to achieve**, leave **all excuses behind** and **know in definite terms that the success that you are pursuing is within sight** because you have **taken the necessary steps** and you have put your plans in writing in an effort to **display your confidence** more vividly within your heart and mind, because you truly believe what you want most will occur because it is divine!

On this day you should now feel confident about what you know, confident about what you will do, confident about what you know you will achieve, and you must now always believe that you will achieve what you conceive!

You can now joyfully wake up and look forward to the day—and future days—due in large part because you committed to changing your ways in a real effort to experience those better days.

When you focus on your circumstances "as opposed to a way out" you are displaying a "lack of confidence" in your future.

On the other hand, when you see your future with clarity you can see and feel the steps that you will take, see and feel reaching those steps and see and feel the improvement in your quality of life.

You absolutely can manage your finances better on a monthly basis, you absolutely can manage your credit better on a monthly basis, you absolutely can improve your finances in all areas throughout your lifetime and **you should feel confident about that knowledge** and the improved financial position that you will soon be in!

By actively managing your finances better you are showing that you are confident and not timid, confident and not fearful, confident and not anxious and confident that what you desire most will come into fruition because you have **prepared for the journey** and **you are sincere** in making the future that you really want to occur—happen in real time.

Your **renewed confidence** and **new approach to lifelong success** provides you the opportunity to NOW operate at a level that is your absolute best!

Chapter 7

Control—*You must know at all times that if you do what you need to do you can control your outcomes*

It is important that you attack your finances in a manner where **you are in control** as the goal—as by doing so you can achieve much more.

Your goal is to solve your financial dilemma before you have a financial dilemma!

And just as those who marched on Washington in the 1960s and dreamed big, so must you also want to dream big and not let others who have a limited dream—put their limitations on you!

You must set boundaries to protect your self-worth and you must know that your self-worth is far more important than your net-worth in the long run.

*When you know **you are in control**, you live up to your expectations of yourself—not others expectation of you!*

In this chapter the importance of controlling the management of your finances so that you can improve upon your finances in "all" areas will be discussed in greater detail.

The Importance of Controlling Your Finances

It is very important that you realize "right now" that you can control your actions now and achieve so much more as it relates to your financial future and the building of wealth.

By gaining control of your finances at the earliest time possible, you can position yourself to acquire more assets during your working years, protect your assets, and gift your assets while you are alive and even after you transition.

What You Gain by Controlling Your Finances

You control your finances by knowing your monthly cash flow, having mastery over how you manage your credit and applying key concepts in the areas of insurance, investments, taxes, emergency fund, education planning, estate planning/wills and retirement planning so that you can set yourself and your family up for a more prosperous future.

You will reach your goals in a timelier manner and that could help free up time so that you can sincerely do what you enjoy and live out your life in a more bountiful manner.

Why You Must Continue to Control Your Finances Throughout Your Lifetime

It is important to have a long-term perspective of why you must manage your finances comprehensively, along with a plan of how you will manage your finances more efficiently.

You must also have a plan in place to periodically review—if you truly desire to make your dreams come true. By doing so you can leave worry, anxiety, fear, frustration, lack of effort and excuses behind you in the wind—exactly where they should be.

Always realize that time is one of the greatest gifts ever given to you—and you have the ability to **control how you utilize your time** as well as **control your daily actions** as it relates to effective management of your finances.

You must control how you respond to adversity so that you can achieve more throughout your lifetime!

You must realize that you can **do far more than you are currently doing** when it comes to the effective management of your finances. You control your thought process, the decision making as it relates to what you are willing to learn and the actions that you will take on a consistent basis.

You control how you will save and invest and address your finances in a comprehensive manner!

You want to get to a point where you "never" discount yourself or what you value—others may be against you, but you don't have to be against yourself, as you **control your actions** and the direction of your future.

By changing your **perspective** about how **you can control your future** you will respond appropriately to adversity and get to your destination faster.

You will face **adversity** along the way—but look at that as being you are that much closer to reaching your destination. You must have the right attitude about things you don't like or things that don't go your way.

You must convince yourself of your ability to control your future!

In spite of the **control over your finances** that you may have (or will soon get), the greatest gift that you can give to others may be your time—and by **controlling your finances effectively,** you can open up more time to "spend" with your loved ones and create memories that will be lasting—primarily because you were in them and you used your time wisely by spending much of it with the ones you love.

Isn't it time you open up a **CAN** of Success by truly deciding to give it your best? You must **c**ontrol your **a**ctions **n**ow so that the success that you desire for yourself, and your family can materialize in real-time!

NOW is the time that you "do more" so that you can open a new door and truly soar!

Your goal is to perform at your best as "you control your mind" and reach a higher level of financial and life success by responding to and managing the adversity that you will face throughout your lifetime.

You must know the scope of your wealth building efforts in advance and by creating your own GPS system you can do just that.

At times in life there will be so much going on and life feels overwhelming, however by having a plan in place that allows you to control your future you put yourself in better position for success.

For those who approach their finances in a manner where they are not in control, the mere thought of managing their finances make them feel very uncomfortable.

It is important that you know the **magnitude or scope** of the financial planning and preparation that you need to do well in advance of doing what you need to do, as by doing so you can smooth out your money management efforts.

And the process can be made easier if you have an approach that puts you in control!

Those who have the eyes of vision, the ears of understanding and a heart of determination to make what they truly desire a reality must do so in spite of how overwhelming life events or world events that they may be experiencing at this time or at any other time—affect their future outcomes in a negative way.

The management of your finances will be made easier over time if you decide to prepare your mind with the knowledge that allows you to "control" the direction that you will travel so that you can move forward with confidence and determination, thereby; allowing you to see the BIG picture of what lies ahead prior to making costly mistakes.

Do you know the importance of speaking appropriately at the right time and listening intently at the right time?

Your goal over time is to <u>operate in a manner that is more favorable to you</u> and you want to learn in advance or control, what you need to do.

You must understand your personal finances during <u>not only</u> the good times; <u>but during troubling times as well</u>, and **Wealth Building NOW** is designed to enhance your understanding of what you need to do and furthermore help you <u>manage your finances in a manner where you don't feel overwhelmed</u> during the process!

Goals

Plans

Success

It is important that you do the right thing for the right reason. It is important that <u>you are intentional in what you do</u> and the <u>opportunity</u> to do and achieve more in your life is now in front of you.

A mindset that allows you to formulate **goals**, **p**lans and **s**uccess principles are what can help direct your future and control the direction that you can go in your life!

It is important to realize that <u>adversity</u> and <u>distractions</u> of varying degrees will be present throughout your lifetime, however it is how you manage adversity and distractions that will occur during your lifetime that are critical for your long-term success.

You will now learn how you can further set **g**oals and make **p**lans that will allow you to achieve more so that you can attain the **s**uccess that will allow you to <u>enjoy life</u> on your terms.

Your goal is to gain the knowledge that allows you to <u>envision a future that is not only realistic,</u> but achievable by you—**if you control** what you need to do.

Goals

Don't let your current level of <u>anxiety</u> or <u>fear</u> limit your ability to<u> dream big!</u>

<u>Address what is trying to counteract or prevent you from achieving more in your life!</u>

You are good enough; you can maintain all that you achieve—if you believe it to be true!

You can set goals that are significant and meaningful to you, so that you are more focused and committed to do what you need to do!

*However, by having a proactive approach and knowing the **magnitude** of what you need to do financially, you can achieve magnificent results and make the big dreams that you now have blossom or come to life!*

Listen to the inspiration within when it is in your best interest to do so, and always set meaningful goals so that you can truly grow.

And always remember to do your absolute best to get through, around or over adversity—as adversity is to be expected when you are going after big dreams.

Whether it be worry, anxiety, fear, frustration, lack of effort, making excuses or any other concern of the mind—body—and spirit—how to conquer what ails you is your responsibility!

Likewise, achieving the goals that you desire most is also your responsibility—as no excuse will do, if you sincerely desire to make your dreams come true.

Plans

What are the actions that can **g**uide you toward the **p**lans that you must put into action that can take you where **s**uccess lives?

You need to have a way of knowing at all times that you must manage your monthly inflow and outflow of cash that comes into and goes out of your household on a monthly and annual basis. You must know the assets that you own and the liabilities that you now have so that you can know your net worth at this particular point in time.

You must have a highly effective system of managing your credit so that you don't become overburdened or overwhelmed with debt in a way that is not healthy and beneficial for you and your family.

Finally, you must have a comprehensive overview of your finances, meaning you know how to address your insurance, investments, taxes, emergency fund, education planning, estate planning/wills and retirement planning in a way that is more beneficial to you and your family—not creditors or others who could care less about your present success—let alone your future success!

Success

Are you in need of <u>re-focusing your thought process</u> so that you can achieve more?

The <u>empowering and enhancing qualities that are needed by you for major success</u> already resides inside of you. You must strive to always attain your goals with righteousness at the forefront—not only when it becomes acceptable to others, but at all times; <u>so that the best qualities that you have</u>—will come to the surface and shine!

Don't be afraid of the after-effects! If you walk in righteousness you will not violate the rights of others and the success that you desire will be more likely to follow <u>at the time</u> that is right for you (pun intended).

You must <u>transform your mindset</u> and the way that you manage your finances. And after you do so <u>it will be too late for others to affect the outcome</u> as you will have pursued the success that you desire in an unrelenting fashion, or another way of stating it— in an <u>intelligent, consistent, and proactive manner</u>

where the outcome highly favors you—because you did what you needed to do!

NOW is the time that you use the **GPS** that you now have at your disposal to achieve at a level that is your absolute best!

It is important to "provide your mind" the knowledge that you need prior to the transaction or the time that you need to use the information for your benefit so that you can have more direction in your life as you will know where you are headed in a more confident way!

As you pursue improving your finances and life, you want to do so in a manner that is uniquely your own!

Do you know your assignment on earth that is uniquely for you or are you a copycat? And does your assignment on earth "really" differ from what others are doing? It is important that you are original in your approach in carrying out your life mission or what you were truly put on earth to do.

By knowing the magnitude of what is required of you with your finances—and your life—you can put yourself in position to avoid financial strife!

Others must not affect you negatively—you are on a mission—going after something—not darkness but light, and you are pursuing what you desire with might, on a persistent basis until you get it right.

You must never be against yourself as <u>that is the role for others</u> who have decided not to operate at their highest level of excellence—let alone <u>control their actions</u> in a manner where it benefits them and their family the most!

Now is the time that you <u>manage your finances optimally</u> and you find your purpose for being here on earth at this particular time so that <u>something can come alive within</u> that will provide you added insight so that you can truly win!

Isn't it time you <u>build a foundation</u> that is earthquake resistant? Even when a **high magnitude** earthquake occurs (major life events), you must remain grounded in the process as the **GPS** that you now possess will allow you to give it your best and go in the direction of your big nest (<u>reaching your retirement number or achieving any other major goal that you may have</u>)!

You have just learned how you can **globally position** your mind for continuous wealth building **s**uccess as you continue to give it your absolute best.

Goals

Plans

Success

Give it your best, as you now have a reliable GPS to guide you toward success! You don't need outward validation of others or the ok from others to start—look within and succeed at a level that is your absolute best again and again—and what you desire most will surely occur in the end.

It is important that you realize that you have the **control within your mind and heart** to chart your future and attain the future success that you desire or the future success that you need to attain.

You must never let failure stop you from attaining your goals as failure is often part of the journey on the path to the success that you need or desire to attain.

Failure will never stop you if you have the attitude that you will get back up and press on and achieve what you desire—regardless of what you face! Your attitude must be that failure is never permanent!

If you stop and think about it—it is often the **fear of failure** or success in some cases that often paralyze those who lack the essential qualities at the right level when they are in the process of trying to achieve their goals.

It is important that you realize that failure is a normal part of the human equation and how you respond to failure is a key aspect of your future success.

You must not look outward and blame others for your failures like so many do! You must "look within" if you want to transform your future into lasting success (big picture perspective)!

You are responsible for the outcomes of your actions and the sooner that you realize that reality the sooner you can start on a path of real success!

If you need to change your behavior or improve in areas where you are weak—now is the time to do so!

Even though your calling may not be in the area of finance—you must still obtain the essentials of what you need to do on a daily basis because you live in a world where the management or lack thereof of your finances is critical.

Your goal should be to **control your mind** and think in an analytical, accurate, careful and critical manner on all matters of significance in your and your family's life on a consistent basis!

Even if you have been disheartened by attempts at managing your finances in your past, you must still have the courage to find a better way that will work for you—so that you can accomplish what you desire or need to do.

However, it is also important that you keep trying and not stop too soon—like so many often do. By **properly controlling your mind** you can do just that.

You must **control your mind** and not concern yourself with how you appear to others unless it is of a positive nature.

Are they attacking you or your behavior? If it is your behavior take the criticism in stride and improve!

If they are attacking, you—disregard the attack and move forward in a powerful manner!

You must get into the habit of **orienting your mind** toward success!

Achieve small goals first (put them in writing if that will motivate you further) and move on to more difficult ones so that you can "build your confidence" and ultimately **orient your mind** toward success.

You are controlling your mind and heart by achieving consistent success!

Most importantly you must **control your mind** to **look at yourself in a positive manner!**

You must feel good about yourself and your future and <u>you must expect success.</u> By doing so you will put your mind in a better position so that you will <u>take initiative</u> and move toward the success that you desire.

Your <u>action and movement</u> towards what you desire on a consistent basis is a proven way of **developing a persistent spirit and orienting your mind toward success.**

NOW is the time that you "control your thought process" and go out and find out what it is that you need to know to achieve the goals that you desire!

You must have a <u>long-term perspective</u> that you will achieve what you desire, even though there may be bumps along the way.

You must have <u>your antennae up</u> for when **the right opportunity** comes your way and you read or hear the right words that you need to read or hear that speaks to your current situation or aspirations.

You must realize that <u>adversity</u> creates opportunity and adversity will often occur in your life to see if you have the staying power to really pursue your goals and achieve what you desire!

If you are now at a point in your life where you truly want success—you must have the mindset that you will have to **control your mind or thought process** if you desire to achieve at a very high level.

You must realize that even though you may now feel that you don't have what it takes to reach your goals—you can still do so.

It is important that you realize that many who at one point on their financial journey felt they did not have what it took—still ended up succeeding in the end! They were able to transform their situation by <u>utilizing many of the empowering principles that can be found in this book,</u> and you can do the same!

It is important that you realize that many consumers have had a difficult stretch in their life at some point and have had to use the control of their mind and taking appropriate action to get through those difficult stretches—and you can do the same.

By **using the control that you have over your mind** you can address what needs to be addressed in your life so that you can <u>achieve the goals</u> that will serve your and your family's best long term interest.

By doing so you can possibly find a way to turn a difficult situation that you may now be in, into that of long-term success in many areas of your life.

Always realize that even though you may fail or have failed in the past—you are not a failure. However, if you stop trying you will become a failure!

It is also important that you understand that your past failures may lead to you discovering your <u>"true ability"</u> and lead you towards major success like many who never gave up did!

You must always remember that **"you have the power to control your mind"** and you don't have to be **controlled** by what has happened to you or what might happen to you in your future.

You can also leave your failures in the past <u>by focusing on meaningful and significant goals</u> and working towards those goals in a <u>diligent manner!</u>

Now is the time that you give it your all, in a controlled and highly committed way—**TODAY!**

Chapter 8

Creativity—*You must know how to use your creativity to achieve even more*

It is important that you realize that you can use your **creativity** to forge yourself and your family forward to <u>accomplish great things in your credit and financial future.</u>

You must realize that if you use your <u>imagination</u> at a high level you can receive the <u>inspiration</u> to do great things while you are here on planet earth.

You have all that it takes inside of you—the question is do you believe it to be true?

By using your mind at a high level and creatively using your mind, you can transform your financial future.

Don't let your thoughts, goals, and dreams be limited by the influence or expectation of others. You possess inside your mind the ability to use your creativity and direct your future!

Do you know that <u>your mind is boundless</u> in the things that you can accomplish in your future?

The key is that you must believe at a high level and <u>take action at a high level</u> to make <u>the goals and objectives that you desire</u> a reality for yourself and your family!

The way that you look at your past, present and future will in large part determine how high you can take your creativity.

If you have had a difficult past, you must leave it there—if your present condition is not ideal you can now transform your position to one of <u>success!</u> If your future looks gloomy at this time, you can now transform that as well.

Transforming your credit and financial future starts with a <u>thought inside of your mind</u> and <u>a real belief within your heart</u> that true success in your credit and financial life can really occur.

Many who have transformed <u>the way that they look at their credit and finances</u> have made tremendous strides in the <u>improvement of their credit and finances—and you can do the same!</u>

You must use the energy that lies inside of your mind and heart to make <u>good decisions</u> and <u>good choices</u> about your credit and financial future.

Once you do that—your **creative energy** will expand exponentially and you will have <u>thoughts and ideas that are inspiring</u> and will take you to a <u>new level of success.</u>

You have access to an ever-flowing source of **creative energy** and now is the time that you tap into it. If you truly want success in your future, you must use your **creative energy** to get to where you need or want to be.

Whether you must use your **creative energy** to find new ways of obtaining income or new ways of looking at your credit and finances—the choice lies inside "your" mind.

You really are the <u>determining factor</u> for creating the type of future success that you really desire and need to attain for yourself—and your family!

Starting today—use your creativity that you were enshrined with at birth to do great things in your credit, finance, and all areas of your life!

Success truly lives on the inside of you, if you believe it to be true!

Having **creativity** means that you operate in a manner where your opinions and thoughts are not swayed or restrained by how others look at you!

You must operate with the freedom to provide the best use of your **creative energy** that is righteous and forward moving to benefit yourself and your family.

By doing so you will start the mental process inside of your mind to attain great heights in your and your family's credit and financial life!

Did you know that if you change your focus and put your vision into action you can see what other minds can't see AND you can create a new reality for yourself and your family?

You must have a system that allows you to see success in your mind first and then put that system in place so that others can see what you see and put what you see in their mind—**so that they can benefit**—if what you have in your mind is of high value **(creative and new)** and can really benefit others!

You must use your creativity and mental focus to improve your credit and financial future to put

yourself and your family in a winning lifetime financial position.

You must <u>activate the thought process within your mind</u> to deeply consider how you can use your **creativity** to improve your living conditions! You must mentally "process and challenge" the material that you are learning in this book—**if your goal is to achieve at a very high level.**

Daily meditation and exercise and the consistent **application of the principles in this book** can help you get your **creative energy** to flow at a higher level!

You will then be in position to use your creativity to move yourself and your family forward in your credit and financial life!

It is important that you realize that the **creation of this book** was the result of **using creativity** to **create** an empowering wealth building book that is designed for your future success **in a comprehensive manner**—in any economic environment!

Be sure to use the principles in this book to change the future dynamics of your credit and financial future in the most empowering manner possible based on your ability to do so.

Now is the time that you use your creativity and <u>other qualities that you have on the inside to reach great heights </u>in your and your family's life!

You have the **creative energy** to do what is necessary to change your and your family's future in a major way.

You must utilize **your creativity** at the highest level possible so that major success is ahead for you and your family from this day forward!

In the current economic environment, it is important that you <u>position</u> or <u>orient your mind toward success</u> as it relates to using your creativity and building your wealth.

And with <u>uncertainty and upheaval</u> running rampant in many areas of society, <u>now is a great time</u> to use your creativity to **orient your mind** to achieve <u>lasting financial success</u>—if you are now ready to <u>give it</u> your absolute best.

The significance of using your creativity will be emphasized due to the importance of why you must use your creativity to **orient your mind towards the goals that you desire** so that you can <u>pursue those goals with more fire</u>—as you reach higher and higher!

- **Determine where you are now at (utilize <u>the 3 Step Approach</u> to properly orient your mind for wealth building success)**

As you ponder your future it is important that you <u>orient your mind for success</u> as you build wealth.

You want to know what your <u>cash flow is and make improvements</u> that may be needed. You want to know what your <u>annual income and expenses</u> are and make improvements where you can. You want to know <u>what you own and what you owe</u> so that you can know your <u>net worth</u> at this time.

You want to use your creativity to know how you manage your credit and how you can possibly do it better!

You want to know how you can analyze and improve upon <u>your insurance, investments, taxes, emergency fund, education planning, estate planning wills and retirement planning</u> as all of that knowledge can put you in a better position for lasting success.

- **Make improvements when you can**

You want to use your creativity to analyze and improve upon your cash flow so that you can increase your cash flow if you need to, cut expenses if you need to—or do a combination of the 2 if you need to.

You also want to improve in the ways that you manage your credit and also improve upon your management of insurance, investments, taxes, emergency fund, education planning, estate planning wills and retirement planning.

By having a mindset of continuous improvement, you can put yourself in position for growth and managing your finances in a more creative and efficient manner.

- **Review on a consistent basis**

After putting into effect plans for improvement of your finances in all areas, it is important that you continuously review to more effectively ensure that your dreams will come true.

By looking at how you have progressed or regressed with your finances, you can get your mind to come up with new ways of looking at and solving financial dilemma's that will undoubtedly occur as you are in the process of building wealth.

While you manage your insurance, investments, taxes, emergency fund, education planning, estate planning/wills and retirement planning—you want to think about <u>creative and new ways</u> in which you can improve in each area at the <u>various stages</u> of your life.

Final Thoughts on Creativity

By **orienting your mind** toward analyzing your cash flow and making improvements when and where you can, analyzing your credit and making improvements when and where you can and analyzing how you manage all areas of your finances and making improvements when and where you can—<u>you will be in a new position and not where you now stand</u>—and you can position yourself to reach a new level of success that will be grand.

*By mastering what you have learned above you can **orient your mind** for success throughout your lifetime as you build wealth and creatively control your financial destiny so that you can enjoy life on your terms!*

And just as app developers use their creativity to create code to direct you in a <u>more focused way</u>—so too must you **orient your mind** <u>(with the right code)</u> so that you can <u>focus on your finances in a more intelligent, consistent, and proactive manner</u> which can potentially better direct you toward what you <u>plan</u> or <u>need to do</u> so that you are <u>on cue</u> toward <u>making your dreams</u> come true!

You must not do like many who <u>manage or mismanage</u> their finances do—**they orient their mind toward failure in ways they don't realize** by letting worry, anxiety, fear, frustration, <u>lack of effort</u> and excuses that they allow inside of their mind and heart do their orchestrated part—rule the day <u>(dominate and consciously or subconsciously control their thoughts and actions)</u> in their lives.

Your goal is to do the opposite, you must see the success that you desire in clear terms and pursue that success as if it has already occurred because you "know" that the success that you are pursuing will be realized!

You must **orient your mind** toward <u>positive qualities</u> that you now have or may need to develop, so that success is more likely to occur—<u>and the success that</u>

you desire rules the day in your life on a more consistent basis!

You must have the commitment, focus, discipline, energy, intelligence and a desire to set goals that you believe in and plan on making happen during your lifetime! And those goals must operate at the forefront of your thought process daily if you are to sincerely reach them!

By doing so you will creatively **orient your mind toward lasting success** that will be yours for the taking if you do what you need to do consistently.

By having the inclination to build wealth more effectively—you can achieve lasting direction as it relates to your finances that provides you a radically different view of how you look at your finances and financial future from this day forward.

Isn't it time that you use your creative abilities to discover what it takes to attain lasting success and isn't it time you direct your thoughts toward true success. Isn't it "time" that you pursue what you are interested in and passionate about at a higher level of intensity so that you can **permanently orient your mind** for a lifetime of success?

Isn't it time you <u>make the decision</u> to see your future with **"clear vision"** so that you can <u>achieve your goals</u> with more precision?

Chapter 9

> **Determination—***Your determination level will determine if you really want the wealth building success that you are pursuing*

It is important that you never let your past stop you from changing your future financial condition or position in a major way.

You must realize that you can recover from anything in your past if you have the will, desire, and **determination** to do so.

You must realize that your **"level of determination"** will be the key in changing your future for the better. You cannot let the opinions of others be an obstacle to you transforming your future for the better.

It is important that you realize that the determination that is needed for true success in your future "must" come from inside of you.

If you have the determination or are determined to cultivate the determination that you now have, this book can help you get on a path to changing your credit and finances for the better.

Your "level of determination" can be improved if you change your thoughts in a manner that blocks out all negative information that you may be hearing from others.

If you look at your life and finances in a different or more simplistic manner you may be able to move forward and accomplish your future financial goals.

Your **determination** and the ability to understand that written goal setting can get you moving in a direction that will lead to you and your family reaching your financial goals in the short, intermediate, and long term—should lead you to seriously consider written goal setting and comprehensive financial planning.

Your level of determination is a critical component of reaching your future financial goals and objectives.

If you lack **determination at the right level**—you may feel that you can't reach your future financial and life goals.

If you are **truly determined** to transform your financial future you must have self-discipline at a high level. By having self-discipline at a high level, you will be in position to follow the written financial plan that you (or your financial planner) create that would actually move you and your family forward.

If you lack **determination** to improve your credit and finances, you are in essence making life far more difficult for yourself and your family. Regardless of where you are currently at financially, you can still improve your finances.

You must realize that "determination" is a "very powerful emotion" and when properly put in motion in a manner where you are truly determined—it has the potential to transform your mindset and put you in position to actually make what you are determined to achieve—a reality.

It is very important that you are truly determined to reach your future financial goals at this time.

If you were once confused or didn't know where to start to "improve" your credit and finances (and you are "truly determined" at this time) you are well on your way to determining in definite terms what you need to do in a manner where you can get started (or continue) on a solid journey of improving your credit and finances for yourself and your family.

It is important that you make the decision today to use the **"determination"** that you have inside of you to really benefit yourself and your family in a major way.

By doing so you can make your and your family's financial dreams come true.

If you desire a yearly vacation that you will truly enjoy, a properly funded retirement, a properly funded education account for your children, being debt free or any other goal that you may have for yourself and your family—you can make it happen if you are **truly determined.**

You must have a high level of determination as you build wealth!

Many who want to build wealth effectively often ask the question of what does it really take to achieve the wealth building success that they desire?

In all seriousness, it is a question that requires a serious answer, and by having the "determination that is needed" you make it easier and more likely to achieve results that will show—and not get an answer to your wealth building question(s) that are most pressing to you that is no—so that you can improve your net worth as you are on the go.

All who truly desire wealth building success or any type of success, not only can <u>achieve the success that they desire</u>—but they can do so efficiently if given the right blueprint for success.

However, your level of success is contingent upon the **"the determination that resides inside of you"** and **"your commitment to learn new and empowering ways of managing your finances"** that can lead to you achieving much more during your lifetime.

How high or big are your dreams of success?

By answering a number of pressing questions of concern outlined below, you can start or continue on a <u>real journey toward wealth building</u> that will have fewer roadblocks and impediments and will help you build wealth more efficiently, and lead you on a <u>clearer path</u> to who you were <u>sincerely meant</u> to be.

Do you know what true determination is?

It is important to know that determination is an "unrelenting spirit on the inside of you" that will NEVER allow you to quit regardless of the obstacles or adversity that you will face.

It is important that you put forward the required effort and you know upfront that obstacles will be in your path (or better yet, put yourself in better position so you reduce the likelihood of facing the obstacle—where possible) and it is up to you to go over, around, above, below or through all obstacles that you face in a manner that says by deed and action "I will never be defeated from achieving what I desire" and by doing so you can not only reach higher you can avoid financial outcomes that are dire!

Many have dreams of success, but when times get difficult, they often welter and fall back into their old habits and by doing so they miss out on reaching a higher level of excellence and learning what their true purpose in life really is.

Don't let that be you!

Are you determined to achieve what you desire?

You put yourself in position to "not letting that be you" by contemplating in a deep manner at this time, what you really want out of life.

If you desire to pay off or pay down your debt at this time, put together realistic plans to manage your finances optimally on a consistent basis in a way that allows you to achieve all of your goals, <u>retire in x number of years</u> and still be able to live your life to the fullest or achieve <u>any other goal(s)</u> that you desire—it all depends greatly on your level of determination.

Do you know foolproof steps that you can take to achieve wealth building success in a way that allows you to give it your absolute best?

By knowing <u>proven steps</u> that you can take to ensure a more prosperous future you can set yourself and your family up for <u>a lifetime</u> of success.

By creating a <u>budget or cash flow statement at a minimum</u>—along with a thorough understanding of <u>your credit</u> and <u>overall finances,</u> you can take your wealth building efforts to a higher level and increase **the determination that you now have** to a level that allows you to prosper.

By utilizing the right system, you will gain <u>the needed insight</u> that allows you to <u>manage your money</u> right. You then put yourself in position to see if you have the <u>potential to achieve</u> the wealth building goals that you desire—and avoid outcomes that are dire— as you move to reach even higher!

You then go out and do it! Are <u>YOU</u> DETERMINED?

Final Thoughts on Determination

Just as a lion has the **unrelenting determination** to catch its prey—so too must you have an <u>unrelenting determination to put in action</u> a plan that can take you towards your goals in a better way!

It is important that you ask the above and other relevant questions as it relates to your wealth building future.

You must have the willingness to do what you need to do <u>even when you don't feel up to it</u> as it is critical for your wealth building success as you journey to find your newly found path that allows you to give it your best.

Why <u>just hope for success</u> or approach what you desire in a <u>haphazard and unorganized way</u> when you have just learned a new and more empowering way—today?

All the best to your **new level of determination** that allows you to achieve at a level that allows you to pass any test.

Chapter 10

Destiny—*Your destiny will be determined by the actions that you take on a consistent basis*

As the final chapter in this book came into focus an appropriate topic to end with became apparent as we are all here to reach (or come as close as we humanly can) our destiny while here on earth.

The topic of reaching your "Destiny" in these difficult times that we now live in is not only an appropriate end point—but something we must always strive for.

In many cases reaching your "true Destiny" requires that you <u>make a commitment at a very high level</u> if your goal is to reach your true financial (or life) **Destiny.**

It is important that you pursue reaching your "Destiny" as it is always a work-in-process as you never truly reach your true **Destiny,** however you want to get as close as possible. If you set the bar high and you take steps daily to get to where you truly want or need to be—whether it be in your financial life (more on that in **Appendix C**) or other areas of your life, you must have a system that ensures you are on the right path.

Your path to your destiny often starts with a simple but sometimes "grand" vision. At no point should you have any doubt that you won't reach your destiny or life purpose!

The success that this book and other books in "The Real Estate & Finance 360 Degrees Series of Books" now enjoy was in effect created on the day that I visualized in my mind that it would occur!

The creation was then followed up with written plans and positive action on a consistent basis.

You cannot just dream or think about it or leave it up to others.

You must be proactive on a daily basis in making your future success happen.

You must always strive to make the goals that you seek materialize during your lifetime!

By striving to do your best in all areas of your life, you too are "destined" for a successful and prosperous future if you do it at a high level.

If you have "true vision" you will have the "inspiration and you will gain the know how" to bring that vision to life yourself—and not rely on the actions of others!

If you don't <u>move to action</u> to bring the vision that you see to life, you might want to question whether or not your vision was true vision and one that will lead you to **your true** destiny.

Even if you don't currently have the <u>know-how</u>—the know-how will come to you as you move to action <u>to make the vision a reality.</u>

If you have "true vision" and you are pursuing your "true destiny" you will be inspired in such a manner that what you see will be brought into existence by you because there can be no other outcome!

You must have the faith and know how to reach your destiny whether it be for your own benefit, your family's or the larger society.

You can reach your **destiny** in your financial life or any area of your life if you believe in yourself strongly enough <u>and you take "real action" to reach your destiny.</u>

To reach **your Destiny** <u>you must not have an attitude of a quitter</u> as failure is always the result of a quitter.

In some cases it may be helpful to stop what you are doing <u>and really think about the goals and future</u> that you want for yourself and your family.

If you pause long enough you may hear your call to "your destiny."

Don't be like many who "hear" their call to their **destiny**—and they never respond!

Don't be like many who "see" their vision clearly—but don't move to action appropriately!

In many cases reaching your destiny <u>requires persistence</u>—reaching your destiny may appear to be a struggle at times, however, you have all that it takes to succeed inside of you—if you focus and plan your road map well in advance.

Don't be a quitter! You must stick it out and be consistent and persistent until you reach or approach your destiny or purpose in your life!

You must be diligent in your daily activities if you are sincere about reaching your **destiny.** In many cases reaching your **destiny** requires that you take risks and get out of your comfort zone.

You must be honest with yourself within your own mind. You must have the <u>fortitude on the inside</u> to persist <u>even when adversity occurs!</u>

To truly reach your "destiny" <u>you must have integrity at all times</u> while you are on your journey, regardless of what others are doing.

Above all **you must have faith** and you must refuse to quit no matter how difficult the task looks or "actually" is.

Even if <u>you have faith in your financial future</u> it is still imperative that you have a <u>written plan</u> that can help you <u>visualize your destiny more clearly</u> and give you the <u>proper focus</u> that is needed so that you can reach your **destiny** more efficiently.

By believing in yourself at a high level, **intellectual thoughts** (at a high level) will be in your midst and you will be able to <u>achieve at a level you never thought was possible.</u>

Did you know that once you <u>"sincerely"</u> make the decision (in your mind) to reach your "destiny or life purpose" you will be led by forces far greater than yourself?

As you begin a serious effort to journey toward your **"life destiny or purpose"** with unflinching <u>determination and effort,</u> you must know that success will be the ultimate outcome!

Oh, one last word of advice—**be sure to set your standards** (regardless of your ultimate destiny) so high that you are in effect "competing" only against yourself. In short, you must do your absolute best on your journey to reaching your goals and **destiny** in life.

You want to "put yourself in position" to have a <u>successful and prosperous</u> future from this day forward by relentlessly pursuing what you desire most!

Your destiny is determined by your decisions—the large and small ones that will play a part in your life forever.

If you take a shortcut today, you may have to re-do the whole project tomorrow! If you fail to take action now, you may be robbing yourself and your family of a more prosperous future.

You must be sincere in your approach, as not being honest with yourself today will lead to you not being honest with yourself tomorrow.

You will more than likely be on a downward spiral where success will be more difficult to achieve—because you did not truly believe.

Final Thoughts on Destiny

It is important that you "persuade yourself" of your ability to achieve wealth building success and truly reach your destiny.

In the times that we now live in <u>many look for others to do what needs to be done</u> when <u>they themselves have the power</u> to do what needs to be done to <u>achieve wealth building success</u> in an efficient manner.

The importance of <u>why you must "fully persuade yourself" of your ability to achieve the success that you desire</u> as it relates to wealth building and achieving in other areas of your life cannot be under-estimated.

You must be convinced of your ability to succeed!

Although <u>this book</u> can be persuasive in getting you and others on <u>a more prosperous path</u> toward wealth building success, **the real persuasion** must <u>begin and end inside</u> of you.

It is important that you cultivate habits of success to a higher level so that you can feel good about yourself and your future.

You can then put yourself in position to develop goals with more clarity and your vision of success will become clearer to you and **you will have more direction** to see your way through, thereby putting you in position to know in more definite terms, what you need to do.

You must put a realistic plan into effect that you believe in! You must have the ability to put a plan that you believe in into "action" so that you can truly reach your goals.

In order to do so you must be **fully persuaded** (within your heart and mind) of the success that you will achieve, because if you are "fully persuaded"— you sincerely believe and you are not hiding anything up your sleeve (you are laying it all on the table and you are pursuing what you really desire at such a high level that there is no doubt that what you desire most will become a reality)!

By implementing plans for attacking your monthly spending and monthly intake of income, implementing plans to have mastery over how you use credit and implementing plans of how you will manage your finances in a comprehensive manner— you are showing that you are on a path to actually persuading your heart and mind to do what is necessary for you to "live more abundantly" and greater success will be much more likely to occur as you embark on your wealth building journey and reaching your destiny.

You must consistently approach your wealth building efforts with confidence.

You must have the ability to create a plan that you believe in and one that you can follow with a high level of confidence and clarity. By doing so you give your heart and mind the ability to move forward at all times—even when adversity occurs.

You cannot have the attitude of a quitter and go in the direction where success does not live as you must have the focus and commitment to see your way through and do what you really need to do, if you truly desire to see your dreams come true.

You must see the success that you will achieve within your heart, you must hear the success that you will achieve within your heart, you must feel the success that you will achieve within your heart, and by seeking to be <u>fully persuaded at this time</u>—you can even get your mind to take part!

The <u>imagination, inspiration, motivation, dedication, determination, preparation, focus, and self-confidence</u> that was put in place to make this book a reality has been overwhelming. However, by putting in the <u>required effort</u> and **having faith,** the blueprint was provided to actually bring this book into existence.

Readers from all walks of life can now benefit and take advantage of powerful systems of credit and finance improvement by using their time and applying significant effort to achieve what they desire.

By having **"faith"** that the book that **I imagined** based on **inspiration that I received** could be created at this time—the **energy to create** such a book occurred in a powerful way!

By seriously cultivating **positive qualities of success** and making a **"sincere"** effort to **put those qualities into action** at a high level, you can make what you desire most occur in a more efficient and effective manner.

It is important that you too, have faith that what you desire most will occur!

You must believe and know that the success that you desire will occur in your lifetime!

Whether your goal is to improve your credit, finance or real estate future <u>or any other goal that you desire</u>, you must really believe that the goal(s) that you set will really occur and **you must have faith** that it will actually occur at the level that you desire!

Part of having **faith** requires that you **move to action consistently** by making the **personal commitment to do what is necessary** to achieve your and your family's **goals and objectives!**

You now have access to **"10 empowering wealth building principles"** that **"you can apply NOW"** and throughout your life to achieve more and build wealth more efficiently.

Adversity—**C**haracter—**E**xcellence—**I**magination—**F**ocus—**C**onfidence—**C**ontrol—**C**reativity—**D**etermination and **D**estiny and how to respond to and utilize those qualities for your and your family's greater benefit now reside inside of you.

The question now is—will you utilize the principles to do what you need to do and make your dreams come true or will you soon forget and not have a clue?

Be sure to use the access to the 10 principles mentioned above that you now have (and inform others) for the greater benefit of yourself and your family from this day forward!

Always remember that if you are truly operating in faith you must have the belief and <u>knowledge</u> **that what you desire will happen in your future!**

You must know that what is unseen (in actuality) in the time and space that now exists will occur in the time and space in your future (will occur or happen)!

You must know **(have faith)** that if you **take the action that is necessary**—you can make it happen in a more efficient manner!

Whether it is improving your credit, finances, real estate, or any other area of concern in your life, you must always have the **"faith"** that what you desire for yourself, and your family will materialize during your lifetime!

By taking action on a consistent basis you are showing that you have "true faith" and you are showing that you are **truly sincere** in your efforts to bring into existence <u>a new and more empowering reality</u> for yourself and your family!

You must realize that you don't have to have a poor state of mind when it comes to your <u>physical, mental, spiritual, intellectual,</u> or <u>financial</u> future!

If you are lacking in any or all of the areas listed above, you must realize fully that <u>"you"</u> can change that NOW!

If you have **poor money management habits**—<u>this book</u> will change the way that you look at and <u>think about</u> your credit and finances <u>and will provide you a new way of thinking that can vastly improve your credit and finances!</u>

You can now find what is missing or lacking in your credit and finances by <u>comprehending and applying</u> what you have learned at your highest level!

*Be sure to use the access that you have to the **10 principles in this book** to your and your family's greater benefit—starting today!*

Always remember, that by applying your faith daily (knowing with certainty on a daily that what you desire most will occur in your future) you can make that which you desire most come into reality much more effectively and efficiently than if you fail to apply your faith daily!

You must also remember that the **10 principles** that you have the opportunity to utilize in your and your family's daily life <u>RIGHT NOW</u> that can move you and your family forward in a highly effective way—was created in large part by **applying faith** on a daily basis.

You must also realize that unlike any other comprehensive financial management system ever created—the **"3 Step Structured Approach to Managing & Improving Your Credit & Finances"** that can be found in **Appendix B** provides you the opportunity to commit to memory and utilize 7 words (actually 5—but 7 is more appropriate) that will provide you a comprehensive approach to <u>attacking your credit and finances on a consistent basis</u> in a highly effective and efficient manner!

Why Having Faith Is So Important

You must realize that this book was brought into existence from a "Vow that was made to God"—to do something great for humanity!

You must never underestimate what God can do in, for, through and around you—during your lifetime!

By utilizing your best efforts to do what is righteous, you can obtain the blessings of God and you will open up <u>endless possibilities</u> for your future accomplishments!

With this book I looked at it as God asking me to participate in what he is doing (spreading personal finance knowledge and success principles to consumers worldwide to their benefit) and my only response that I could come up with was a resounding—YES!

When God is working on major change in your life you will often not know what is going to be created down the line!

Something big (a pivotal moment where you dig in and make a serious commitment to do what needs to be done) will often occur in your life to show others God's true power.

You must remember that if you are called to do something (your life purpose) you are already equipped with what it takes to succeed!

However, you must think and know that you are equipped by taking **direct action** on a consistent basis—if you are to get powerful results!

Why You Must Dream Big

You must realize that if you **dream big** and receive and act on **the powerful inspiration** that comes your way—God will always be with you in whatever he called you to do!

You must find your passion and purpose in your life if you are to **achieve** at your highest level.

Many would have thought it impossible or improbable that a book that provided all that you received in this book could be created in an efficient manner—with powerful content that could truly move you forward.

However, by having the faith all along that it could and would occur and by having a big imagination— that which was needed to bring this book into reality occurred in a powerful manner!

What You Must Do Now

We ask that you make a real commitment to see your future clearly and act on making what you see a reality—if it is in your best interest to do so!

If you dream big and pursue more in your life—you will receive more in your life! **You must really go after your goals and dreams at this time!**

Be sure to use **your faith** <u>along with all of the other success qualities that you may need to cultivate to a higher level</u> to take yourself and your family to where you need or want to be in the most effective and efficient manner possible during your and your family's lifetime!

It is my belief that the <u>content in this book</u> is an instrument of God's Glory and bigger than what I thought or what I imagined this book to be when it was conceived!

This book is a testimony of the success that can be attained by those who truly believe and those who are willing to take the <u>necessary action</u> to bring what they desire into reality in a <u>sincere manner</u>—to benefit themselves, <u>their family</u> <u>and society</u>!

You must remember that you must always approach life in a <u>proactive manner</u>—not re-actively (to prevent times of trouble or adversity from occurring) when approaching your credit, finance, real estate or any other area of your life.

God can use you to do great and mighty things if you open your mind up to the possibility and you give all the glory to God.

It is important that you realize fully that God can use you in a big way—TODAY!

By **utilizing your faith** and <u>taking decisive action</u> all of your dreams are possible!

Below is a song that I was inspired to create that I feel sums up my and my family's life that has helped **direct my faith** on a daily basis.

If you find benefit in it—utilize it to stay positive and reach your goals or your destiny.

You Were the One

You were my THEN and my NOW—my WHEN and my HOW!

It was you right from the start—who dwelt in my heart!

Through your power and your glory
—you told your story!

It was you right from the start—who dwelt in my heart!

As I reach back in my mind from my very first thoughts—I realized that it was you!

By the power of your love—you showed us the miraculous!

You showed me—what I could truly be!

By your grace—I can now clearly see that it was you right from the start—that dwelt in my heart!

You showed me the impossible!

You showed me the remarkable!

You showed me the incredible!

You showed me the improbable!

It was you right from the start—who dwelt in my heart!

You were my THEN and my NOW—my WHEN and my HOW!

It was you right from the start—who dwelt in my heart!

The above poem was inspired by gospel singer Joe T. Adams song "It Was You" off his Breakthrough Album and in a real sense the above poem or song states how I feel about **faith.** If you find some benefit in it, be sure to use it in your life to reach your highest heights and achieve the level of success that you desire!

When it comes to applying your faith, you must always believe that something greater is coming if you prepare your mind properly with the right knowledge and you take the right action—consistently!

You must understand fully that nothing significant will happen if you fail to **move to action** as you embark on your journey—whether it be improving your credit and finances or attaining any other goal or purpose in your life.

Why accept a lower standard of living or not reach significant goals in your life when you don't have to?

*Use **your faith** to make what you desire most—occur!*

You must "really" have **faith** that what you desire will occur in your future for the greater benefit of yourself, your family, and society!

Are you now ready for the test?

All the best to your future success....

You are now equipped for wealth building success if you are willing to give it your absolute best—**NOW!**

Sincerely,

Appendix A

10 Additional Topics to Further Ensure Success

In the paragraphs below you will find **"10 helpful tips that came to mind as I was finalizing this book"** that can help you achieve your financial (and life) goals at a higher level "in this and the coming decades" while you are here on planet earth.

- **Know what to avoid**

It is important that you manage your finances from a standpoint of understanding **what** you need to avoid.

You cannot let worry, anxiety, fear, frustration, and lack of effort dominate your mental space.

By purchasing this book and frequenting **www.TheWealthIncreaser.com** and other wealth building sites, you are showing a real commitment for successful outcomes to happen in your future.

- **Know what to confront**

In a similar manner to knowing what you must avoid in order to achieve optimally—you must also know what you need to confront. You must prepare your mind for success by gaining the right knowledge and using that knowledge appropriately.

You must not only have that knowledge—you must actually confront **your current cash flow position, your credit understanding and your financial understanding in all areas**—if you desire to achieve optimally throughout your lifetime.

- **Have a big imagination**

How do you approach your finances and financial future? Do you even have an approach?

Nothing can hold you back more than your inability to dream big—and pursue those big dreams!

You must formulate significant goals and **have every intention within your mind** of achieving those goals.

By **thinking about your future and what lies ahead by dreaming big,** you put your heart and mind in position to receive the vibration and rhythms of life that can lead to "life happenings" going your way.

- **Begin with the end in mind**

You must begin with the end in mind whether it is a car purchase, home purchase, educational goals, retirement goals or any other goal.

By doing so you put yourself and your family in a more favorable position for success.

Will I sell or trade in my vehicle in 3 years?

Will I stay in my home for 20 years and then move to my dream location?

Will I begin saving now to help fund my child's educational needs 15 years from now?

Will I allocate my risk profile with my investments in an appropriate manner? Will I sell stock X that I bought at $5 per share—all or in part—when it hits $20 a share?

Will I choose mutual funds, or will I use a stock portfolio to help reach the goals that I desire—or will I use a combination of investment vehicles to reach the goals that I desire?

Will I save appropriately so that I can reach my "retirement number" so that I can do what I desire in my retirement years?

The above—and **other probing questions** based on the goals that you are pursuing are what you must ask and answer on the front end—so that you won't suffer on the back end!

- **Always know the importance of your credit score**

A good score generally starts at around 700 and the higher you go after that point the better.

You get into the great or excellent range once you score 750 or higher and that would put you in position to get the best rate in most transactions that involve credit.

Your **mastery of the 5 credit factors** that you have already learned in this book and will further learn in **Appendix B**, will position you for the increased success that you desire or need to achieve at the various stages of your life as it relates to your credit and credit score.

- **Keep your monthly bills under 10 so that you can win**

You must make it a point to manage your bills monthly (mortgage, auto loan, gas, electric, water, garbage, phone, cable, and credit cards) at an optimal or highly effective level.

Keep in mind that if you are at nine bills or twelve bills you are still ok—the goal is 10 or so per month—to add clarity to your mind and thought process so that you reduce stress on a daily, monthly, and annual basis.

You must have **clarity** and **focus** on a daily basis and not allow clutter to cloud your mind!

By keeping the number of bills that you pay from your checking account on a monthly basis **under 10**—you set your living circumstances up so that you can win.

This success principle does not mean that you can't have other accounts to reach your ultimate goals such as an account for entertainment and living outside of your "fixed monthly expenses" or investment accounts and other accounts that are designed to help you reach your goals.

- **Know your money management personality**

By knowing how you manage your finances on a daily, weekly, monthly, and yearly basis—you put yourself far ahead of those in the general population who go about their daily activities in a manner where they don't have a clue.

Are you a **highly effective money manager**—or do you need to improve?

There is no need to panic as you can achieve lasting success regardless of your money management style.

- **Know where you are at in your life stage**

Whether you are just entering the work force, just graduating from college—or you have been working for years—it is important that you understand **the stage in life** that you are at.

By doing so you add clarity to how you see your future and you make reaching many of your goals more likely to occur.

- **Always establish a properly funded emergency fund**

It is imperative that you **establish an emergency fund** at the earliest time possible, and properly fund that emergency fund.

By doing so you help reduce the future risks that you will face in your life and success will be more likely to occur.

- **Have faith that what you are pursuing will truly occur**

You must know and act consistently in a manner that says to the universe—I will succeed!

You must **sincerely pursue the goals that you desire** so that you can give your mind added incentive—to reach higher!

You must <u>believe and know</u> that the results that you are pursuing—will show!

It is important that you use your **experience, expertise and you exercise the use of your mind in a spirit of excellence** if you desire to <u>achieve more</u> during your lifetime.

And just as "that process" led to the creation of three leading financial blogs, <u>numerous books and e-books</u>—and increased profitability for <u>Realty 1 Strategic Advisors</u> and <u>TFA Financial Planning</u>—so too can you use that process to make big things happen in your life.

Even though the **year of 2010** (my first year of blogging) started on an upbeat note with the creation of <u>www.the-best-atlanta-real-estate-advice.com</u> and later that year <u>www.realty-1-strategic-advisors.com</u>, the author of **Wealth Building NOW** would face great adversity in the spring of 2010 when the mentor of the creator of **Wealth Building NOW** transitioned and even greater adversity later that same year when the younger brother who looks just like the author of **Wealth Building NOW** unexpectedly transitioned in the fall of 2010.

Those unfortunate events tested the faith of the author of **Wealth Building NOW,** however by responding positively to adversity in the same manner as I have urged you to do in this book—the continuous development of a number of sites took on a new meaning and increased urgency—and brought forth over 700 pages of web content that you can now benefit from <u>at this time along with the creation of a number of books in "The Real Estate & Finance 360 Degrees Series of Books" that are now on the market</u>.

Always realize that the success that you desire often begins by looking within and giving **serious thought** to what you desire most in your future.

You must leave "all" <u>excuses or reasons why you can't reach your destiny</u> behind you, so that you can take the necessary steps toward making your dreams come true.

You must open your mind up to the inspiration <u>(and always be open to receiving inspiration when it is in your best interest to do so)</u> that will follow and you must have a strong desire on the inside of you—to make your dreams come true.

That <u>initial thought at a deep level</u> can lead you on a journey toward making the right moves <u>at the right time</u> and more effectively guide you toward your destiny!

In the end (or maybe the beginning depending on where you are now at) it is your timing, your willingness to move to action, your preparation, your focus, and an unstoppable belief on the inside of you—that will guide you in the direction of doing what you definitely need to do—to make your dreams come true.

Use what you were enshrined with at birth (a spirit of excellence) while you are here on planet earth!

It is of the opinion of the author of **Wealth Building NOW** that this book will act as a springboard to success and will help you achieve many of your financial goals.

However, you must realize that the opinion of the author of **Wealth Building NOW** is biased in favor of the author.

You must determine for yourself whether **Wealth Building NOW** is the best book for you—or whether there is another book on the market that will work better—as far as making your dreams come true.

Always remember that the burning desire that you have on the inside at this time (or at some time in your future) to do "something big" may be the voice of God giving you the "ignition" that you need to help direct your steps and give you added strength to bring something new and powerful into this world—

at a time and in a manner that is uniquely designed for you!

I leave you with a poem that can hopefully inspire you to do more throughout your lifetime.

Use the poem to reach your highest heights to truly be all that you can be!

INSPIRATIONS FOR MOTIVATION

Greatness is not going to come to you!

You must take it to greatness in order for that to be true.

Look at the stars and the moon.

And you too will be there soon.

Aim High!

And—you too will exceed the sky.

As you meditate and ask God, how far can I go?

And he'll reply—only you know.

Within all of us is the ability to take it to levels never before seen.

Or are you going to settle for the average mean.

The future is yours, only the heavens know how far you will go.

Will you give it your all or are you only show?

God loves you—will you give it your all?

Or will you stay at your same level and remain small.

You owe it to yourself for being in existence.

To always strive higher—and be persistent.

All the best to your continued success in the next ten years in your life—and beyond...

Appendix B

The 3 Step Structured Approach (A Comprehensive Financial Management System)

In easy-to-understand format, you must know how to implement the 3 steps below if you desire to manage your finances optimally:

1) <u>Utilize personal finance statements appropriately</u>

1. Establish a personal **b**udget or cash flow statement at a minimum
2. Create a personal **i**ncome statement
3. Create a personal **b**alance sheet
4. Create a personal **n**et worth statement

2) <u>Gain mastery of how you manage your credit</u>

Negative information must be kept off of your credit report

Utilization of your available credit must be at a reasonable level

Time of open accounts is important

Type of accounts are important

Inquiries must be kept at a reasonable level

3) <u>Comprehensively understand your finances in the following areas</u>

Insurance

Investments

Taxes

Emergency fund

Education planning

Estate Planning/Wills

Retirement planning

By just being **exposed to** the **3 steps** above—you are far ahead of the average consumer who for the most part has no real understanding of what personal finance encompasses—let alone the ability to use the knowledge of what personal finance encompasses to their and their family's greater benefit.

What you need to do financially

Now that you have knowledge of what you need to know (pun intended) **you must take the right steps** and put into action the results of your cash flow statement or budget at a minimum. Whether you have a monthly surplus or a monthly deficit <u>you are now in position for more effective planning</u> from this point forward.

If you are comfortable with numbers, you may also want to create an <u>income statement</u> and <u>balance sheet</u> so that you can determine your <u>net worth</u> at this time—and improve upon your net worth in the coming years.

The creation of a <u>"properly funded emergency fund"</u> will go a long way in helping you increase your net worth in future years!

You must also gain mastery over how you manage your credit by knowing how to **utilize your knowledge of the 5 credit factors**—as that knowledge can prevent you from getting into a difficult financial hole where climbing out is <u>difficult or highly unlikely</u> (you may need to <u>consider</u> filing bankruptcy as a real option).

Finally, you must know how to select the appropriate insurance products and investment options along with doing, education planning, estate planning and retirement planning in a manner that is more advantageous for you and your family—not creditors or others who have no real concern for your lasting success.

The importance of reviewing what you do financially

Now that you have a comprehensive overview of your finances and you have been **exposed** to all that you need to know (and do) to work toward making your wealth building goals come true, you "must" be aware of your need to review!

You must review your personal finance statements, including your emergency fund to make sure you are adequately protected. You must review your understanding of the 5 credit factors so that you can make the right or at a minimum, good decisions as it relates to your use of credit.

You must review your insurance, investments, taxes, emergency fund, education planning, estate planning/wills, and retirement planning on a routine basis to see where improvements can be made.

Regardless of your past experiences, the environment in which you grew up in and the positive or negative exposures in your life, you are now in position to change all of that to your advantage—and by being **exposed to personal**

finance in a way that you can readily understand and utilize, you are now ready to take your prize.

It is important that you are **exposed to all areas of financial planning** that you need to do throughout your life at the earliest time possible. By doing so you can get out in front of potential disruptions and "proactively plan your future" in a manner that is more advantageous for you and your family.

You can put yourself in position where you can live with confidence and the success that you desire will not only occur—it will be expected. You no longer need to approach your financial future with doubt, uncertainty, and a feeling of "can't do"—as by purchasing this book you have positioned yourself in a major way to make your dreams come true.

All the best because of your willingness to be "exposed to financial systems" that can lead to lasting success.

The 3 Step Structured Approach to Improving Your Credit & Finances®

Step 1

BIB N

You can easily remember BIB N

B—stands for Budgeting or Cash Flow Statement

I—stands for Income Statement

B—stands for Balance Sheet

N—stands for Net Worth Statement

The above statements are all personal finance statements, and you will need to create and analyze each one. Be sure to be as accurate as possible with the data you enter.

Once analyzed, you will have to determine ways that you can improve each statement and then come up with a written plan of action for improving each statement so that your financial ratios and net worth will move in the right direction.

Step 2

Remember **NUTTI** or **MUTTI** in your GUTTI to improve your credit score forevermore.

This too, you can also easily remember:

N stands for Negative Information—**M** is for Messed Up--If either occur, your credit will be highly affected as this generally makes up 35% of your credit score.

U stands for Utilization or how you use your credit, and it too is very important as this generally makes up to 30% of your credit score.

T stands for Time and is another important factor as you should keep older accounts open and always pay on time. Just as "i" in time comes before "y" in type, time comes before type when you are memorizing this acronym. Time generally makes up to 15% of your credit score.

T stands for Type and it comes after time. The types of credit you have are important as a good mix is better than no mix. If you have several credit cards, a home loan, and an auto loan that would be a better type of credit than just having several credit cards. The type of credit makes up to 10% of your credit score.

I stands for Inquiries and you should keep your inquiries low if you will be seeking new credit and/or are attempting to improve your credit score. Inquiries also make up to 10% of your credit score.

Note the descending order of the percentages above are:

N or **M** = 35%

U = 30%

T = 15%

T = 10%

I = 10%

Total 100%

Remembering in that order will also help structure the acronym so keep the percentages along with what each acronym represents fresh in your mind.

If your credit is unsatisfactory at this stage, you will have to clean up your credit and work on getting your credit position to an acceptable level so that you can reach your future goals and objectives.

Step 3

My Eyes Tear

My Eyes Tear when I see that my financial future is clear.

The above sentence is a play on words and the memory triggering aspect is:

Your eyes would represent the (**ii's**).

Your tear would represent the (**teeer**) in the following acronym.

The first (**I**) represents your Insurance Planning

The second (**I**) represents your Investment Planning

The (**T**) represents your Tax Planning

The first (**E**) represents your Emergency Fund

The second (**E**) represents your Education Planning

The third (**E**) represents your Estate Planning/Wills

The (**R**) represents your Retirement Planning

You will have to analyze each area of your finances and see what you need to do immediately and, in your future, to improve your position. You should also know at this point what you will need to do in the future as you may not be in financial position now to address all your financial concerns.

However, you should be aware at this stage of what you need to do in "all areas" of your finances.

Now, do you think you can cultivate a mental framework or mindset that includes the **3 steps above**?   Of course you can!

OK, Let's Review

- **BIB N** stands for…

- Remember **NUTTI or MUTTI** in your GUTTI to improve your credit score forevermore and each letter in **NUTTI and MUTTI** stand for…and the percentage in each letter stand for…

- **My EYES TEAR** when I realize my financial future is clear and **your eyes are your (ii's)** and **your tear are your (teeer)** and each letter stands for…

Recite it in your mind until all the "3 Steps" become second nature to you. Don't get too concerned about the deeper understanding of each letter at this time as they will come to you if you navigate www.realty-1-strategic-advisors.com and/or you purchase **Managing & Improving Your Credit & Finances for this MILLENNIUM**—our new book.

Additionally, it will all come together for you by navigating **TheWealthIncreaser.com**—our most recent blog site.

With just what you have just learned you put yourself ahead of most consumers when it comes to the effective understanding of personal finance.

This is only the beginning of your journey to financial freedom. Just mastering and understanding the 3 steps listed above are well worth the price you paid for this book, as you now have the essentials of what you can do in your future to attain lasting success.

Open your mind, ears, and eyes wide as we go into deeper detail of how you utilize **The "3 Step Approach" to Managing & Improving Your Credit & Finances** in your and your family's life—today!

Get your "mindset" to the point where for the rest of your life you will always know:

BIB N—Remember **NUTTI or MUTTI** in your GUTTI to improve your credit score forever more—and my **EYES TEAR** when I realize my financial future is clear.

Once you have the above acronyms solidly memorized you will be well on your way to living your life in a manner that suits you and your family best—not your creditors.

Be sure to comprehend the above acronyms at your highest level. In other words, open your mind, ears, and eyes wide and put on your thinking cap.

In this appendix you can master your understanding of credit and finance in a style and manner rarely seen—in personal finance.

This appendix was intentionally written in a somewhat entertaining and engaging style with serious content that was designed to get your mind to open.

By reading this short book you should be in great position to apply the information and change your and your family's financial condition for generations.

Final Thoughts on The 3 Step Structured Approach

It is critical that you have the proper understanding, and you know how to properly apply the helpful acronyms that you have learned.

You must at all times know:

1)

that you need to properly create and analyze your **B**udget or Cash Flow—so that you know your inflow and outflow of cash monthly.

Even if you decide to create an **I**ncome Statement, **B**alance Sheet Statement and **N**et Worth Statement later—you need to create at a minimum a Budget or Cash flow Statement—at this time!

2)

Your understanding and application of Remember **NUTTI** or **MUTTI** in your GUTTI to improve your credit score forevermore.

Improving Your Credit Score in a Nutshell

Remember **NUTTI or MUTTI** in your GUTTI to maximize your credit SCORE, FOREVERMORE!

Follow me here...It will make sense...I promise...

N---"Negativity"---try to avoid negative information in your payment history---35% of your score

U---keep "Utilization" and amount owed low---keep debt low---30% of your score

T---always pay on "Time," keep old accounts open---15% of your score

T---keep a good mix and have different "Types" of credit---10% of your score

I---keep "Inquiries" low by loan shopping within a small window---10% of your score

Or Another Way to Look at It

M---don't "Mess up" your credit---try to avoid "negative info" on your report---35%

U---keep "Utilization" at a low percentage of your total debt---keep debt low---30% of your score

T---always pay on "Time," keep old accounts open---15% of your score

T---keep a good mix and "Type" of credit---10% of your score

I---keep "Inquiries" for the last 12 months low if you will be seeking new credit---10% of your score

Did you know that I set you up for a short catchy Acronym (although somewhat strange) that has the potential to help you take control of your credit for the rest of your life?

If you memorize and utilize the following phrase in the right manner, you will be in position to improve your credit position. Feel free to pass it along to your family and friends to help them improve their credit score and credit situation as well.

Although the Acronym (memory trigger) is somewhat "weird" you should easily remember it for the rest of your life by reciting it in your mind on a constant basis—until you are confident that you have it memorized, and you understand the underlying concepts behind the acronym.

Remember NUTTI or MUTTI in your GUTTI to maximize your credit SCORE, FOREVERMORE!

By simply memorizing the preceding Acronym—and utilizing the knowledge gained—you can take positive control of your financial situation—and that of your loved ones.

OK—one last time...

N stands for ... and M stands for... 35% of your score

U stands for... and U stands for...30% of your score

T stands for... and T stands for...15% of your score

T stands for... and T stands for...10% of your score

I stands for... and I stands for...10% of your score

OK, your time is up, I'm sure you have all the factors that go into maintaining and improving your credit and credit score mastered.

It is also important that you realize that there are two major credit scoring models:

1) FICO score
2) VantageScore

If you utilize the five factors above appropriately you will have a good to excellent credit score regardless of the model that is being used. Always realize that newer models, older models, industry specific models and other models are on the market at the same time and the calculation of your scores will vary depending on the model used by the creditor or the entity requesting your score.

Furthermore, you should know that there are 3 major credit bureaus:

1) **T**ransUnion
2) **E**quifax
3) **E**xperian

An easy way to remember the **3 major credit bureaus** is to think that you will be **TEE**ing off— however it won't be for golf—but for improving your credit and credit score!

The above structuring technique brings clarity to help you improve and maintain you credit for the rest of your life. By simply remembering the weird poem or statement—you put yourself in position to always know what you need to do to improve and maintain your credit.

It is also important that you realize that consumers who must concern themselves with the FCRA (Fair Credit Reporting Act) and other corrective credit improvement systems—normally are those who have mismanaged their credit in the past.

It is imperative that you manage and improve your credit and finances in a **more intelligent, consistent, and proactive manner**—to avoid getting into a credit position that is adverse for you and your family!

You can choose to learn other creative ways or even learn the FCRA standards and guidelines and other systems of credit and finance management if you choose too—however I do not believe you will find a more effective and efficient system than "Remember **NUTTI or MUTTI** in your GUTTI to improve your credit score forevermore"—that you have learned in this precise and to the point guide.

However, do not use my belief—**as an excuse** to not do your due diligence and determine for yourself if there is a better system or approach that is available that will work better for you and your family.

It is imperative that you use your intelligence to analyze other credit and finance systems in an **analytical, accurate, careful, and critical manner** and decide for yourself what works best for you and your family!

If you comprehend and master the use of "Remember **NUTTI or MUTTI** in your GUTTI to improve your credit score forevermore"—you will primarily have what you need—to succeed when it comes to managing and improving your credit for the rest of your life.

It is important that you realize that the **"3 Step Approach"** and the Credit Improvement system mentioned above—will essentially provide you with what you need once you get your credit properly established.

If you desire a comprehensive system that can move you forward on a continuous basis—you have found that with the "3 Step Approach."

Therefore, don't get too uptight or concerned about your credit as long as you have a thorough understanding and you know how to apply in a practical manner (and you actually do so)—"Remember **NUTTI or MUTTI** in your GUTTI to improve your credit score forevermore."

Be sure you understand and remember the **ratio percentages** for each letter as by doing so you will be well ahead of 90% of the population when it comes to the understanding and application of credit.

And having the ability to maintain and increase your credit score on a consistent basis is an important skill set that you can pass along to others.

Be sure that you understand that different jargon may be spoken or written regarding the credit factors mentioned above, and it is your responsibility to understand that jargon.

By mastering the **"3 Step Approach"** you will even have a more effective and efficient practical system of credit and finance management and understanding than many professionals who work in the financial industry.

You can choose to waste or perhaps not waste your time by learning about the FCRA (Fair Credit Reporting Act), CFPB (Consumer Finance Protection Bureau), USA.gov—and other credit resources that may add more confusion and frustration than lasting results, or you can choose to know and use "Remember **NUTTI or MUTTI** in your GUTTI to improve your credit score forevermore"—and use the knowledge that you have gained in a manner where you will apply what you have learned to manage and improve your credit in a more stress-free, effective, efficient and results oriented manner!

You can choose to remember that your worthiness, character, capacity, and general reputation plays a major factor in your credit score. It is important that you choose to **"properly focus"** and leave excuses behind—and by comprehending and applying "Remember **NUTTI or MUTTI** in your GUTTI to improve your credit score forevermore" on a consistent basis you can put yourself in position to manage your credit effectively for years to come.

You also should know that by mastering "Remember **NUTTI or MUTTI** in your GUTTI to improve your credit score forevermore"—that does not preclude you from learning additional credit systems and approaches.

However, you must realize that it is truly not necessary for your and your family's future success if you operate in a proactive (gain the knowledge that you need NOW—by using the above acronym in a way that is most beneficial to your credit usage or anticipated credit usage) manner!

It is important that you realize that the amount of credit that is made available to you is often based on the income that you earn in your household and other factors.

It is also important that you realize that your failure to understand how to manage your credit and finances is your choice and you must further realize that you are responsible—not only for your future success but the success of your family and other loved ones as well!

If you have an established and functional **(mental working knowledge)** system of attacking your credit and finances, you can more precisely and more accurately determine what lies ahead (plan better) for you and your family in the financial realm of your and your family's life!

You must live your life purposely and with a real willingness to achieve what you desire!

A **comprehensive system of approaching your credit and finances** leaves nothing to chance—and is an approach that those who truly desire success utilize on a consistent basis!

3)

The final structuring technique in the **"3 Step Approach"** that can help you improve your finances is listed below.

My EYES TEAR

- My eyes tear when I see that my financial picture is clear.

- My eyes tear when I see that my financial independence is near.

- My eyes tear when all my credit card balances disappear.

- My eyes tear when I realize I have no financial fear.

- My eyes tear when I know that I have succeeded this year.

If you were to look at the above poem on the surface it would have some meaning to you. However, the real power of the poem lies beneath the surface— and when properly applied could easily change your mindset or the way that you look at finance in general.

Acronyms can play a key role in simplifying complex problems and can make the mind work easier and eliminate or reduce your stress levels.

In the above poem your **eyes** are your (**ii's**) and your **tears** are your (**teeer**). Let me explain further so that you have a clear understanding.

The above poem is a "play on words." In your financial life you should be concerned with your **i**nsurance and **i**nvestments or another way of looking at it your **eyes (ii)**.

In your financial life you should also be concerned with your **t**axes, **e**mergency fund, **e**ducation planning, **e**state planning/wills, and **r**etirement planning or another way of looking at it your **tear** (**teeer**).

- By simply remembering the poem above or simply the title of the poem—you bring clarity to your financial understanding immediately.

- By reciting the poem or a line in the poem **daily, weekly, monthly, or whatever time frame you prefer** you get to a point where you know <u>all of the areas of your finances that you need to address immediately</u>—thus reducing your stress level—or concern about your finances.

- Used in conjunction with **BIB N**, Remember **NUTTI or MUTTI** in my GUTTI to improve my credit score forevermore—**my eyes tear** when I see that my financial picture is clear has the real effect of **"you knowing all of the areas of**

your finances that you must address" at the drop of a hat!

- This alone would greatly reduce the stress in your life and give you a feeling of well-being in your financial realm for the rest of your life—**particularly after you address and improve each area to the maximum effect possible based on your financial condition**—and you can address those areas more appropriately at this time by going to www.realty-1-strategic-advisors.com—NOW—and/or purchasing **Managing & Improving your Credit & Finances for this MILLENNIUM**!

- Although what you have just learned are simple concepts—by reciting and understanding the concepts behind what the acronyms stand for you have immediately brought clarity to your credit and financial life and that alone would put you well ahead of the general population as far as understanding your credit and finances.

- You have just had the opportunity to master these life-changing acronyms—keep them in the forefront of your mind as you go through life—as by doing so you will improve your and your family's credit and financial future well-being—significantly!

Can you believe that a **"3 Step Approach"** that utilizes **7 words**—has provided the mental framework that allows you to know in a **comprehensive manner—what you need to do for the rest of your life** to manage your credit and finances in a highly effective and efficient manner?

However, don't take the above statement at face value! You must seriously ask yourself—do I have a system that does the above—or do I know of a system that does?

Appendix C

Thomas (TJ) Underwood Author/Blogger

Thomas (TJ) Underwood has created over 700 pages of credit, finance, and wealth building articles covering the entire spectrum of personal finance on three websites.

The three sites have brought forth a new version of financial planning that turn the odds in your favor (not creditors) and more importantly puts you in control of your finances and wealth building activity in a way that could lead to greater success for you and your family throughout your lifetime.

With 2010 being the year of "when the blogging career of Thomas (TJ) Underwood all started" and 2014 year of **TheWealthIncreaser.com** being created and 2024 being the **ten-year anniversary** of blogging on **TheWealthIncreaser.com,** along with 2024 being the year of the **10th book** in "The Real Estate & Finance 360 Degrees Series of Books"—the author of **Wealth Building NOW,** has provided insightful principles and approaches to wealth building that could further lead to you achieving lasting success.

In the **preceding chapters** and **appendices,** you have learned about **10 success principles** that can transform your life if applied appropriately and can help you achieve your financial (and life) goals at a higher level "in this and the coming decades" while you are here on planet earth.

In the **BONUS SECTION** you will learn an **Investment Simplification & Wealth Building approach** that can easily take you to where you need or desire to go so that you can truly achieve results that will show.

In addition, be sure to visit the following sites to enhance your wealth building knowledge even more to achieve optimally throughout your lifetime:

TheWealthIncreaser.com

Realty-1-Strategic-Advisors.com

The-best-atlanta-real-estate-advice.com

BONUS SECTION: Investment Simplification & Wealth Building

Learn how you can at this time choose the right investment vehicle(s) to effectively reach your investment goals.

It is important that you start your <u>long-term investing</u> at the <u>earliest time possible</u> and there are <u>investment vehicles</u> that you can utilize to get you where you need to be more efficiently.

In this **bonus section** you will learn about some of the most useful and time-tested investment vehicles that you can use to build wealth and reach goals that you desire at the <u>various stages</u> of your life.

Your path to **investment success** does not have to be a difficult one if you start early, invest consistently and you know your "target number" that you need to reach to fulfill your various goals.

Your home purchase, college funding, traveling around the world, reaching your <u>retirement number</u> or reaching the number that you need to reach for any other purpose is attainable if you are <u>at this time</u> willing to make a <u>serious effort</u> toward achieving what you desire.

Mutual Funds (MFs)

A **Mutual fund** is an investment program funded by shareholders that trades in diversified holdings and is professionally managed. It normally includes a "bundle of stocks" and investment products and frees you from the hassle of selecting individual stocks or other investments yourself.

A **MF** is a portfolio of stocks, bonds and other securities and creates a diversified investment portfolio that generally reduces your risk factor. It is key that you understand that mutual funds are "**bought and sold**" at the **"end of"** the trading day!

- Mutual funds are sold based on dollars, so **"you can specify any dollar amount"** that you'd like to invest.

- Mutual funds are divided into several kinds of categories, representing the kinds of securities they invest in, their investment objectives, and the type of returns they seek. Although there are others, most mutual funds fall into categories which include **stock** funds, **money market** funds, **bond** funds, and **target-date** funds.

- Mutual funds charge annual fees, expense ratios, or commissions, which may affect their overall returns and you want to ensure that the fund that you select has reasonable fees.

- Employer-sponsored retirement plans commonly invest in mutual funds and if your employer offers them--especially with an employee match, you want to put yourself in position to contribute as best you can, based on your financial ability to do so.

Index Funds (IFs)

Technically a Mutual Fund, **Index funds** invest in stocks that correspond with a major market index such as the S&P 500, Nasdaq, or the Dow Jones Industrial Average (DJIA). It could be one focused on a sector, such as healthcare, durable goods, or technology. This investment strategy requires less research from analysts and advisors, so your expenses as a shareholder would be lower, and these funds are often designed with **cost-sensitive** investors in mind.

- The positives of index funds are that they require little financial knowledge, are low cost, and are convenient to invest in. On the negative side, you could end up stuck with poorly performing assets and the potential for returns to be less than those of successful managers of actively managed funds.

- The goal of index fund managers are to mirror the performance of a particular index – and not try to outperform it, which is the goal of managers of active funds.

- Although many think that index funds are relatively new, the first publicly available index fund was launched back in the mid-1970s.

- Index funds **often perform better than actively managed funds over longer** investment time frames. Even so, there are still risks involved with this style of investing. If the tracked index falls, then your investment's value will follow and if it is at the time of your retirement or planned withdrawal, you will suffer financially, and your living conditions could be affected.

- You can reduce risk by diversifying your portfolio by holding several different index funds covering a variety of stock markets or sectors.

- Index funds can provide a very straightforward, cost-effective, and diversified way for you to steadily increase your wealth over time. Fund managers do not decide which individual investments they should buy or sell, which is what happens in active mutual funds.

- *Investors in these products expect their chosen index to rise over the long term, even if it encounters some turbulence along the way! The performance of the FTSE All-World Index, which has delivered an average annual return of 9.3% since 1993, according to Vanguard, provides a real world blueprint (30 plus years of results) of what index funds can achieve IF utilized appropriately.*

- So, should you as a novice investor choose an active mutual fund(s) or index fund(s)? You can spread your risk by investing a portion in each at the level that you are comfortable with. Again, index funds replicate the performance of an index, whereas the managers of mutual funds will pick and choose securities they believe will help them outperform that index. If an active manager makes the right calls, then they can substantially outperform their benchmark index and deliver handsome returns to investors--normally with more risk.

Popular index funds that you may want to consider include the following:

*Fidelity 500 Index Fund (FXAIX)

*Schwab S & P 500 Index Fund (SWPPX)

*T. Rowe Price Equity Index 500 Fund (PREIX)

*Vanguard 500 Index Fund Investor Shares (VFINX)

*Many others

Be sure to do your own independent research, confirm that fees are low, and you can do so by going directly to the sites by "typing in the ticker symbol" using your favorite search engine!

Target Date Funds (TDFs)

Although technically a mutual fund, **target date funds** are separated out in this discussion in order to give you more clarity on how you can use them to build wealth.

Target-date funds are a "set it and forget it" or "invest it and rest" retirement savings option that removes two headaches for you as an investor:

1) deciding on a mix of assets which saves you time and

2) re-balancing your investments for you over time which saves you time

Target-date funds, also known as **life-cycle funds** or **target-retirement funds**—aim to continually strike the right balance between the risk necessary to build wealth and safer options to protect a growing nest egg.

The fund automatically re-balances your portfolio with the right mix of stocks, bonds and money market accounts as you age and is a great hands-off way for you to build wealth if that fits your personality and risk profile!

Target Date Funds are "mutual funds" that **purchase from other mutual funds** (known in the "investment world" as a "fund of funds") and they are designed to build a diverse portfolio. While you set and forget or invest and rest so to speak, the fund updates your asset allocation over the years for you.

Early in your working life, a target-date fund generally is set for growth by having a much larger slice of your portfolio in stocks rather than fixed-income investments like bonds, which are safer but provide smaller returns (the approach is similar to that of a 529 education savings plan). As your retirement year approaches, the fund gradually shifts toward more bonds, money market accounts and other lower-risk investments.

Your retirement year is the "target date" of most of these funds--unless you choose a target date for other purposes, and the funds are conveniently named to correspond with your planned retirement year. Say you are 35 years old and plan to work until you are 65, a Target Date 2055 would possibly be of appeal to you. Most target-date funds are named in **five-year increments with some at 10-year increments,** so you would choose the provider with a fund named with the year nearest your planned retirement date or other target date based on your goals.

Below you will find some of the more popular target date funds that you may want to consider:

Fund

Vanguard Target Retirement 2045 Fund Investor Shares
Fidelity Freedom Index 2045 Fund Investor Class
Lifecycle Index 2045 Fund Premier Class
American Funds 2045 Target Date Retirement Fund Class R-5
T. Rowe Price Retirement 2045 Fund

There are many other target date funds, and the current data is current as of market close on February 1, 2024. Be sure to do your own independent research as the accuracy of the data cannot be guaranteed.

Always realize that the main appeal of target-date funds for most is their simplicity. And just as an index fund operates with simplicity, so too does a target date fund!

The funds go from a "high ratio" of riskier equity funds to safer investments like bonds, and money market accounts as it gets closer to the "target date," **freezing your asset allocation** to protect your nest egg.

An important question to ask yourself or your advisor when choosing among target-date funds is whether the account will freeze the year you plan to retire, or whether a "through" fund that continues the glide path for 5, 10, 15, or 20 years past retirement before freezing your asset allocation will be in effect. You want to plan your approach appropriately and select the fund that's right for your retirement or other goals.

How to purchase:

*through your retirement plan

*directly from fund

*open brokerage account ($500 to $3,000 to open)

Exchange Traded Funds (ETFs)

They are similar to **Mutual Funds** as just a few key differences set them apart. The biggest similarity between **ETFs** (**E**xchange-**T**raded **F**unds) and mutual funds are that they both represent professionally managed collections **(or "baskets")** of individual stocks, bonds or other investments.

*However, investment minimums are normally lower with an ETF! You can purchase an ETF share of **Vanguard FTSE Emerging Markets** for under $100. Many more ETF shares start at $500 or more, and you can learn more about ETF offerings by visiting <u>VettaFi financial</u> website.*

- It is key that you understand that **ETFs** allow you to trade **"throughout the trading day"** at market prices. This flexibility **is a key difference** in how the **fund** works as compared to a mutual fund. This level of flexibility may be utilized by active traders making moves throughout the day.

- The main difference between ETFs and mutual funds are that an ETFs price is based on the market price and is sold only in **"full"** shares. Mutual funds, however, are sold based on dollars, so **"you can specify any dollar amount"** that you'd like to invest.

- As an investor, **you have options** and can reap the benefits of diversification.

When you are investing you must know that your goals, risk-tolerance, income and your personal situation must also be taken into serious consideration.

If you currently owe $100,000 on your home mortgage and you desire to pay it off in 5 years, you will need to do some analysis and not just choose the first thing that comes to your mind. If your monthly payment is $1,000 and $500 of your mortgage payment is going toward principal, in 5 years your balance would be roughly $70,000 if you continued that path.

By adding $1,200 to the monthly payment of $1,000 you could pay $2,200 monthly ($1,700 going toward your principal) and have your mortgage paid off in 5 years, however you would be responsible for paying your property taxes (mandatory) and insurance (optional after your home is paid off, but generally makes sense to have).

Or you could choose an investment strategy of investing the $1,200 per month for 5 years in the market and based on historical trends you could have over $90,000 after 5 years, and since you continued your mortgage payments at $500 per month in principal payments, you would owe $70,000 and therefore have an addition $20,000 plus after the payoff of your mortgage, in your pocket by doing so—assuming your returns were as expected.

In this example inflation is assumed to be 3% and your rate of return is assumed to be 9%. Even if you only assumed a rate of return of 3% (same as inflation) you would have over $80,000 which would still put you ahead by over $10,000 after the payoff of your mortgage. As long as you had a positive return you would come out ahead based on the assumptions mentioned above.

If after 5 years of investing you had a negative return you would possibly fall short of the $70,000 that was needed and you could decide to ride the market longer and pay off the mortgage later, cash in, in spite of the losses and payoff as much as you could on the mortgage.

*As you can see from this discussion, your goals, risk tolerance, income and personal situation will play a large part in **how you decide to pay off your debt** and how you select your investments!*

You want to know how to invest properly on the front end and you want to know that you can **invest inside of your retirement account(s)** (your earnings will grow tax free) and avoid taxes for years or **outside of your retirement account(s)** (you will provide 1099 and other paperwork to your tax professional that your brokerage would send to you at tax time) where you would possibly owe taxes on an annual basis (ETFs and Index funds are often tax efficient even outside of retirement accounts).

If you are age 25 and desire to **retire by age 55** with your house paid off and **over 4 million** in your account in today's dollars, you would have to invest $1,600 monthly for 30 years assuming 3% inflation and a 10% rate of return—and also assuming you pay your house off within that 30-year period.

Therefore, in the above examples, your returns would be affected depending on the type of investment and whether the investment is inside or outside of your retirement accounts. Once you reach age 59 1/2 you can withdraw your retirement funds without incurring an early withdrawal penalty, however you would pay taxes at your ordinary income rate—unless the distributions were from a ROTH IRA or there was an exception that applied.

Mandatory withdrawals from your traditional IRA or retirement plan would be required once you reached age 73, however with a ROTH IRA, there are no mandatory withdrawals, however after your death your beneficiaries must take required minimum distributions!

Also realize that you can choose **balanced funds** that invest in a hybrid of asset classes, whether stocks, bonds, <u>money market</u> instruments, or alternative investments. The objective of this fund, known as an asset allocation fund, is to reduce the risk of exposure across asset classes.

In closing, it is important that you realize that this discussion is not about theory or what you possibly need to do, but <u>what you **CAN**</u> do! You must at this time <u>analyze your income and expenses</u> and determine your <u>discretionary income</u> that you have available so that you can start investing now, get more income by creating a plan to increase your income whether by the <u>payoff of your debt</u>, scaling back on your entertainment and other expenses—or finding other ways to get income on a consistent basis.

Although you will hear many financial planners tout the fact that you can increase your savings and come up with a significant amount to invest by scaling back on the $5 that you spend daily on your favorite latte or coffee, that is not something that we are a big proponent of as we realize that for some, a $5 cup of coffee can give them the added energy that is needed to help them earn more on a daily, weekly and annual basis—therefore they more than offset the $100 or so that they spend on a monthly basis on coffee that they could be using for investing.

However there are <u>other ways</u> that you can <u>get more income and cut expenses</u> and you may want to analyze and pursue them!

Once you determine the amount of income that you have available to invest and you commit to investing that or another amount over a "period of time" **you can start on a path to reaching the number that you need to attain your goal(s)** and live daily with <u>more joy</u> on the inside!

Whether your discretionary or available funds to invest are $200 per month or $2,000 per month and you decide to use it to invest long-term, you can achieve significant results over a 30-year period.

By calculating what you can do now, **(you need to know your discretionary or available income that you have to invest, whether you will invest weekly, monthly, yearly or a one-time lump-sum investment and furthermore you need to know the "time frame that is needed or desired" to reach your goal)** you can determine the nest egg that you can have by investing consistently in a relatively painless way—starting today.

Investing $200 monthly at 3% inflation and a 9% rate of return will give you over $500,000 (five-hundred thousand) in 30 years!

The 4 percent raise that you get, the promotion that you get, or working one or two days a month for lyft, uber, grubhub or other new economy options can easily provide you that cushion to invest either temporarily or permanently over the next 30 years.

In many cases, you can find the $200 by analyzing your monthly spending and tightening up your budget some. You can do a detailed analysis of your insurance products, taxes and other areas of your finances and discover new savings or increases in income. The ways that you can come up with the needed funds for long-term wealth building success is endless—if you want to achieve your goals in a sincere manner!

Investing $2,000 monthly at 3% inflation and a 9% rate of return will give you over $5,000,000 (five million) in 30 years!

To get that extra $2,000 per month you may have to start a business, have your stay-at-home spouse find employment either part-time or full time or determine other ways to increase your monthly income based on your creativity and the unique skills that you now have or will cultivate in the near future.

In many instances high net worth and high-income earners wasted hundreds if not thousands on a monthly basis on frivolous or unnecessary spending that could be utilized more appropriately for building long-term wealth of significant amounts.

What is the **discretionary amount** that you "need or want to get to" so that you can invest at this time and in your future, to work towards making life more manageable for you and your loved ones?

How You Can Invest using Mutual Funds, Index Funds, Target Date Funds and Exchange-Traded-Funds:

1. Make sure you have a brokerage account with enough cash on hand, and with <u>access to mutual fund shares and other investments</u>
2. Identify specific mutual funds or ETFs that match your investing goals in terms of risk, returns, fees, and minimum investments. Some brokerage platforms offer fund screening and research tools.
3. Determine how much you want to invest initially and submit your trade. If you choose, you can set up automatic recurring investments in the amount that you desire.
4. Monitor and review performances periodically, adjusting as needed.
5. When it is time to close your position, enter a sell order on your platform.
6. Realize that with some funds you can invest directly and depending on the fund type, the functions mentioned above will be done by the fund manager or brokerage.

While many mutual funds are no-load (no sales charge), you can often avoid brokerage fees and commissions by purchasing a fund directly from the mutual fund company instead of going through an intermediary or third party. Expense ratio is the percentage of your account that is calculated for the fund management such as .20 expense ratio on a $200,000 fund would mean you are paying $40 for the fund management and that would have the effect of reducing your fund amount by $40 for that particular year, or if held in a retirement account the ratio would accumulate from year to year and would be subtracted out from your funds once you were to retire or cash out.

There are pros and cons of investing utilizing mutual funds and you can go to investopedia.com to learn more about investing in a simplified, yet effective manner!

Some funds are defined with a specific allocation strategy that is fixed, so the investor can have a predictable exposure to various asset classes. Other funds follow a strategy for dynamic allocation percentages to meet various investor objectives. This may include responding to market conditions, business cycle changes, or the changing phases of the investor's own life.

The portfolio manager is commonly given the freedom to switch the ratio of asset classes as needed to maintain the integrity of the fund's stated strategy.

Below you will find what is often included in mutual funds, including balanced funds, index funds, target date funds, and exchange traded funds.

Money Market Funds

The money market consists of safe, risk-free, short-term debt instruments, mostly government Treasury bills. An investor will not earn substantial returns, but the principal is guaranteed. A typical return is a little more than the amount earned in a regular checking or savings account and a little less than the average certificate of deposit (CD).

Income Funds

Income funds are named for their purpose: to provide current income on a steady basis. These funds invest primarily in government and high-quality corporate debt, holding these bonds until maturity to provide interest streams. While fund holdings may appreciate, the primary objective of these funds is to provide steady cash flow to investors. As such, the audience for these funds consists of conservative investors and retirees.

International/Global Funds

An international fund, or foreign fund, invests only in assets located outside an investor's home country. Global funds, however, can invest anywhere around the world. Their volatility often depends on the unique country's economy and political risks. However, these funds can be part of a well-balanced portfolio by increasing diversification, since the returns in foreign countries may be uncorrelated with returns at home.

Specialty Funds

Sector funds are targeted strategy funds aimed at specific sectors of the economy, such as financial, technology, or health care. Sector funds can be extremely volatile since the stocks in a given sector tend to be highly correlated with each other.

Regional funds make it easier to focus on a specific geographic area of the world. This can mean focusing on a broader region or an individual country.

Socially responsible funds, or ethical funds, invest only in companies that meet the criteria of certain guidelines or beliefs. For example, some socially responsible funds do not invest in "sin" industries such as tobacco, alcoholic beverages, weapons, or nuclear power. Other funds invest primarily in green technology, such as solar and wind power or recycling. Fidelity Charitable and other "Socially Responsible Investment Funds" are now available in abundance in the investment world.

Other

Bond, precious metals, natural resources, crypto and other investment products are now packaged and sold as mutual funds in some instances.

You can **use the above approaches** to ensure you reach your "retirement number" or "other goals" that you have—and use other riskier or more aggressive approaches to further build wealth if you are in position to do so.

Investing a **percentage of** your investments in mutual funds, index funds, target date funds and ETF funds can be a painless and simple way for you to build wealth and live out your retirement with dignity. Automatic Investing (dollar-cost averaging) $200 monthly in a mutual fund, $200 monthly in an index fund, $200 monthly in a target date fund and $200 monthly in an ETF fund **(total of $800 monthly)** will provide you a hefty return over time if market trends continue. You can also invest $200 per week and invest automatically if you feel that will work better for you.

The above approaches, along with your social security and possibly pension income can put you well ahead of most, if you start early and invest consistently. You no longer have to fake it until you make it, you can now be true to yourself as you are now on a serious path toward making your dreams come true, because you decided to take your mind off the shelf!

Isn't it time that you use a "more pragmatic approach" toward investing and building wealth?

Always realize that you have **numerous options** to choose from in the investment world regardless of your goals, however the process of **investing in an effective manner is not that complicated,** unless you make it complicated. In this short (relative to what you have learned) bonus section you have learned how you can invest in a straightforward manner and achieve realistic results that can enhance your living conditions while you are here on planet earth.

All the best to your investment and wealth building success...

Thomas (TJ) Underwood is the Real Estate Broker at Realty 1 Strategic Advisors, LLC—one of the most successful real estate and financial planning companies in the metropolitan Atlanta area. Realty 1 Strategic Advisors is based out of Peachtree City, GA.

He is a former fee-only financial planner and top producing loan processor, and he has assisted clients from as far away as Germany with their financial concerns. The concepts in "Wealth Building NOW" have been utilized by savvy consumers to help them build wealth and achieve many of their major financial goals.

He is also the creator of TheWealthIncreaser.com, one of the leading financial blog sites that can be found in the internet universe.

Wealth Building NOW

10 Principles for Wealth Building Success

ISBN: 978-1-953994-22-6

Publisher: TFA Financial Planning

Email: tj@TheWealthIncreaser.com

Currently **The Real Estate & Finance 360 Degrees Series of Books©** *consist of:*

Book 1) Managing & Improving Your Credit & Finances for this Millennium
Paperback **Copyright© 2012**

Book 2) HOME BUYER 411 *The Smart Guide to Buying Your Home*
E-book **Copyright© 2014, 2023** Hardback **Copyright© 2023**

Book 3) HOME SELLER 411 *The Smart Guide to Selling Your Home*
E-book **Copyright© 2014,2023,** Hardback **Copyright© 2023**

Book 4) The Wealth Increaser E-book **Copyright© 2014,** Hardback **Copyright© 2023**

Book 5) The 3 Step Structured Approach to Managing Your Credit & Finances E-book **Copyright© 2014, 2023** Hardback **Copyright© 2023**

Book 6) The FIZBO Manual (For Sale By Owner Guide) E-book **Copyright© 2014, 2023** Hardback **Copyright© 2023**

Book 7) 1-2-3 Credit & Me E-book **Copyright© 2021, 2023** Paperback **Copyright© 2023,** Hardback **Copyright© 2023**

Book 8) Credit & Finance Improvement Made Easy E-book **Copyright© 2014, 2023**

Book 9) Wealth Building Axioms E-book **Copyright© 2024,** Paperback **Copyright© 2024**

Book 10) Wealth Building Now E-book **Copyright© 2024,** Paperback **Copyright© 2024**

www.ingramcontent.com/pod-product-compliance
Lightning Source LLC
Chambersburg PA
CBHW030934220326
41521CB00040B/2312